LLAMA BABIES: UP,DRY, AND NURSING

Acknowledgments

The events described in this book would not have happened without the efforts of my husband, Curt Anderson. He is my partner on the farm, sharing its joys and disappointments. He encouraged me to write this book. His computer expertise made bringing it all together possible.

Thanks go to my sister, Margaret Norris Doherty, for her assistance in editing the manuscript.

Disclaimer

LLAMA BABIES:
UP, DRY, AND
NURSING

BARBARA NORRIS ANDERSON

A+ LLAMAS

Llama Babies: Up, Dry, and Nursing

Copyright © 1996 by Barbara Norris Anderson

All photos by Curt and Barbara Anderson

ISBN:0-9654791-0-2
Library of Congress Catalog Number:96-086675

Published by A+ Llamas Publishing, 6238 Inwood Lane South,
Salem, OR 97306
Printed in the United States of America

Contents

INTRODUCTION

Welcome to our farm. In this book you will see us grow from a small operation with six weanling llamas to a medium sized breeding farm. This is the story of ten years of llama babies.

Curt and Barbara Anderson (that's us) fell in love with llamas in July of 1984. We were driving through Grants Pass, Oregon, when we happened to see a sign at the fairgrounds announcing an upcoming LANA Llama Expo. We juggled our trip so that we could attend on Sunday, the last day. That decision changed our life. We came home and put our house up for sale. We were moving to the country where we could have llamas. We wanted to start with two pack llamas. Barbara began shopping for llamas. Pack llamas were not to be found. By September we had purchased six weanlings, three females, and three males. We traded our house in town for one in the country. By November, we moved in. The llamas arrived with the furniture.

We did not give up our day jobs. Curt teaches math and computers and Barbara teaches special education. The llamas did not make us rich monetarily in the twelve years we have been together, but they added a richness to our lives we never anticipated.

Our farm is located a mile south of the city limits of Salem, Oregon. It sits on the side of a hill, in a clearing in the woods. Level ground is at a premium, even with thirteen acres. It was once part of a fruit farm, evidenced by old walnut, apple, and cherry trees. Most of the shade is provided by Douglas firs, maples and oaks. We have a wonderful view from the house. We can see most of our pastures, our large pond, the neighbor's horse pasture, the woods, a tree farm, a grass seed farm and a baseball diamond. The house is in the middle of the property. The barn is near the house, but up the slope. The section of the property nearest our lane is too steep and wooded for llama pastures. A stream runs though the bottom of the ravine. Several natural springs also feed the pond. We use this area for training trails. In 1994 we purchased nine acres of almost flat land just up the road from us. It includes a large arena we use for training. Most of our males now live there.

Having both grown up in Los Angeles, we had to learn about living in the country and raising large animals. The farm is like having a second full time job. Throughout the years, we have operated under a few guidelines:

1. Learn everything we can about llamas.
2. Operate the farm like a business.
3. Use the best veterinary services available.
4. Have fun with our llamas.
5. Contribute to the llama community through active participation in the Willamette Valley Llama Association.
6. Work hard and play hard.

The stories in this book are told as they happened. They were not changed to hide the bad or to put our farm in a better light. Look closely and you will notice the growth. In most cases, the names of the llamas have been changed. All our llamas are sold with full disclosure, so changing the names does not benefit A+Llamas. In fact, I had to omit all my fun naming stories. I changed the names to avoid inadvertently hurting someone. To rename so many llamas, I took the names out of the WVLA directory and assigned them as I wrote. Names are included simply to help the reader track the animals through the story.

We hope you enjoy your visit to our farm.

CHAPTER 1 - 1986

September 22, 1986 Alan: First Born

Dam's Name:	*Gretchen*
Baby's Name:	*Alan*
D.O.B.:	*9/22/86*
T.O.B.:	*about 1 p.m.*
Sex:	*male*
Weight:	
BoSe:	*yes*
Navel:	*Iodine*
Hernia?:	*no*
Teeth:	*all four*
Heart & Lungs:	
Temperature:	
Weather:	*sunny*
Problems / Comments:	

The first cria is a big event. In our case, since we started with six weaning llamas, it was long in coming. My husband, Curt, says the only way to start slower is to buy geldings. Gretchen, the oldest of the three females, was the first to get pregnant. We had tried breeding her to our young male, but it did not take. A neighbor offered the services of her elderly herd sire, Hershey. We loaded two of our girls into our VW van and drove the two miles to her farm. We left Gretchen outside in a pen and took Tammy inside the barn to the stud. Luck does odd things. Omar, my friend's other male, leaped over several fences and bred Gretchen while we were inside. Our luck, it took with one breeding.

Gretchen was due in late September, after the start of school. We would be back to work. My parents decided to come up from California and baby watch. My dad grew up on a farm in Arkansas. He had lived and worked all his adult life in Los Angeles until he retired to Atascadero. He was slightly amazed that his youngest daughter, Barbara, was living on a farm. Visiting us was nostalgic, sort of back to childhood. He figured llamas could not be any different from cows and horses. Surely, at seventy, he could still do the job.

Our herd was up to eight llamas. Hershey and Omar had joined us after a family crisis had caused my friend to move. Hershey had become permanently lame. A goat had broken his hip when he tried to mount her. He was our yard llama, moving around on three legs. We live on a hillside. Hershey usually stayed in the yard or driveway where it is almost level. Our fencing was far from adequate. We had been putting up new fencing in our spare time since we moved in. However, I think we were still in the slow learner phase. The girls' pasture had a good solid field fence installed under the direction of my dad. The rest was a hodgepodge of many different styles. At the bottom of our property was field fencing separating us from the neighbor's horses.

The folks knew something was up when the boys started screaming at one another. Gretchen was out in the middle of the girls' pasture. Hershey was watching her from the other side of the fence in the driveway. The other four males, including Omar, now gelded, were in their pasture when mom and dad went out the driveway to look. Sure enough, two feet and a nose poked out of the birth canal. Suddenly, chaos broke loose. The boys were out. Chaucer, our biggest male, now two and a half, attacked Hershey. The five males raced up and down the driveway, around the house and into the back yard. Hershey jumped the fence into the lower pasture to get away. Fence jumping is not easy on three legs. Hershey tumbled down the hill, not stopping until he hit the fence at the bottom. He did not move. He could not. All four legs had gone through the field fencing. He was trapped.

Dad had to choose between the baby and old Hershey. He left Mom to watch Gretchen and headed to the garage. Armed with fence pliers, he climbed to the bottom of the slope. It took him most of an hour to extract Hershey from the fence. Hershey was cooperative, but little help. Gravity seemed to be working against them. First Dad cut loose the section of fence. Then he had to cut Hershey free one leg at a time. By the time Dad got back up the hill, the baby was born and up nursing.

When I got home at four, everything was under control. Dad had already spliced in a new section of fence. Mom was in heaven telling of the birth that Dad had missed. Curt and I went out to the barn to see our new baby boy, Alan, a beautiful soft gray. Curt dipped the navel in iodine. Our llama neighbors from down the road and over the hill came over to help give the BoSe shot. We had entered a new phase of our llama career.

I want to add a comment about the BoSe. Although we had located and were using a llama vet, I had picked up the BoSe shot from our local farm vet. Included in the syringe was some thick yellow stuff. I asked about it. The old time farm vet said it was vitamin D because anything born in the Willamette Valley needed Vitamin D supplementation. He did not see that llamas would be any different. It took nine years for the llama community to recognize that piece of knowledge.

BoSe vs. MuSe

BoSe and MuSe are selenium supplements. Never give MuSe to a cria. It is so concentrated that it is fatal even in 1cc doses. Do not even keep it around. Once it is injected, death is certain. If you need to use it on your adults, have your vet do it or figure out some way that it never be accidentally administered.

Now that I have your attention, BoSe is given in areas that are selenium deficient like the Willamette Valley. It is not given in areas that are selenium high like the Central Valley of California. Check with your veterinarian.

CHAPTER 2- 1987

April 15, 1987 Irene: The Princess

Dam's Name:	*Mary*
Baby's Name:	*Irene*
D.O.B.:	*4/14/87*
T.O.B.:	*daytime*
Sex:	*female*
Weight:	
BoSe:	*yes*
Navel:	*Iodine*
Hernia?:	*no*
Teeth:	*all four*
Heart & Lungs:	
Temperature:	
Weather:	*sunny*
Problems / Comments:	

Irene was our first Chaucer daughter. Mary, her dam, is solid white, with a beautiful white mane. Chaucer, the sire, is white with a large brown spot and black eye patches. We were surprised to get a solid dark brown llama out of two white parents.

Irene was born on a sunny spring day while we were at work. We drove up the driveway to see two long brown ears sticking up through the tall green spring grass. Curt went out and picked her up and carried her down the hill into the barn. Mary followed, humming, and occasionally trying to give Curt a body block. We dipped the baby's navel in iodine and gave a BoSe shot.

Tammy, one of our other females, coveted Irene. She wanted that baby for herself and kept trying to steal her away. We worried that Tammy would confuse Irene and interfere with mother baby bonding. We shut Tammy out of the barn and kept Irene and Mary inside until Irene had nursed several times. It did not take more than a day for Irene to be able to recognize her own mom. Tammy became a favorite aunt.

Irene was the little princess. She was the center

of our little female herd. Alan was never allowed to play rough with her. If he so much as hinted rough play, one of the girls would rush over and reprimand him. She was never left alone. Someone was always at her side. She was the star of evening romps.

Irene grew up to be our very best mom, out producing all four of our initial females. Her children paid our bills. Her efforts supported our llama herd. If all llamas were like her, the llama business would be a dream.

So far our first two babies were born in the middle of the day just as we had been told they would. Both were problem free just like we had been told. Would they make us rich like we had been told? Would I be able to retire early and raise llamas? Were all those promises really true?

Iodine

Iodine is one of the products used to dip the umbilical cord and navel. It is no longer the first choice in a situation where repeated applications are possible over a period of two days. Iodine comes in several concentrations, seven percent is the one to use for this application. Iodine is corrosive. If it is stored in a baby box, the lid must be tight. It is a good idea to place the bottle in a second sealed container. The fumes from the bottle can ruin the contents of the baby box. Iodine can ruin any jewelry it contacts. That means do not wear rings when using it. Iodine burns. It hurts the cria if it gets all over the baby's skin. Iodine literally seals the germs in, as well as keeping things out. It dries up the cord quickly. Iodine stains everything, too. Wear rubber gloves while dipping the navel with iodine to avoid burning and staining the hands.

September 11, 1987 Alice: Lost Teeth

Dam's Name:	*Gretchen*
Baby's Name:	*alice*
D.O.B.:	*9/11/87*
T.O.B.:	*daytime*
Sex:	*female*
Weight:	*30+*
BoSe:	*yes*
Navel:	*Iodine*
Hernia?:	*no*
Teeth:	*not fully erupted*
Heart & Lungs:	
Temperature:	
Weather:	*sunny*
Problems / Comments:	

Alice, our second Chaucer daughter, arrived 354 days after her brother, Alan. Since Gretchen was rebred in October, floppy eared Alice was probably a little early. She was a big baby, over 30 pounds, but her teeth were not fully erupted. She was born with capped ears. The sack or epidermal membrane had held them plastered down to her head. Like the first two, she came while we were at work. Her life was uneventful until we tried to wean Irene.

In spite of the 5 month difference in age, Alice and Irene were great friends, almost inseparable. In October, Irene was 6 months old, ready to be weaned. Gretchen had weaned Alan herself, but Mary was not about to wean the little princess. We asked around about weaning strategies. After Gretchen weaned Alan, we simply put him out in the yard. He got to be our next yard llama. During the summer he saw plenty of action following us around as we worked. He could visit with everyone. We needed a different plan for Irene. It would be winter soon. She needed company and shelter. We ended up splitting our little herd, putting Irene and Tammy in one pasture and her mother, Gretchen, and Alice in the other.

Disaster hit on the morning of day two. We went out for morning chores. The girls came running up to the barn as usual. Alice saw Irene running towards her and ran to meet her, slamming into the field fence separating the two pastures. I did not realize the consequences right away. I saw it happen. I saw her hit. I saw her shake her head. I thought she was okay.

The next day I knew we had a problem when I found a tooth protruding through the side of Alice's cheek. We hauled her to the vet's. I felt sick holding an injured month old baby in my arms. Upon examination and x-ray, we found out that Alice had knocked out or broken all her teeth. Tooth shards were everywhere. The vet carefully removed all the pieces. The ragged stumps were extracted so she could nurse. The cuts all had to be stitched. Had she damaged the tooth buds? Would she get normal permanent teeth? Would she get adequate nutrition?

Alice was a beautiful llama. Ears were now erect, I had hopes to show her. So much for that. You can not show a llama with no teeth and expect to win.

Some months later, Alice's jaw was x-rayed again. This time the x-rays were examined by Dr. Chuck Forrest, an orthodontist and llama breeder who had taken an interest in Alice's problem. The tooth buds were there and developing normally.

Today, Alice is nine years old. Her teeth are in good shape and her bite is perfect. She does have an annoying habit of rolling up her upper lip and not pulling it down over her front palate. It makes her look like the raspy old llama on the Banana Republic t-shirts. Could it be the scar tissue?

Floppy Ears

Many llama babies are born with floppy ears. It is true that the ears of premature babies flop, but so do many full term ears. Usually the ears stand up within two weeks. It can take time for the cartilage to firm up.

Floppy ears can be taped into shape. Moleskin can be used on the inside for support. A soft plastic rod such as the ones used for permanents can be taped inside for support. Do not tape in cold weather because it increases the possibility of frostbite.

In Alice's case, we put moleskin inside her ears to stiffen them. Then we used adhesive tape to form them into a more desirable shape. She looked like a Doberman with freshly cropped and taped ears. We kept the tape on for about two weeks. Since then we discovered leaving the ears untaped gets very similar results. Most ears do stand up after about two weeks even if you do not tape them.

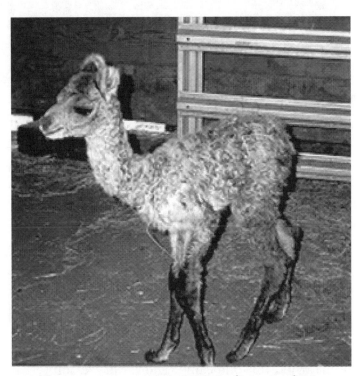

Floppy ears may take two to four weeks to stand up.

December 10, 1987 Opal: Fat Mama

Dam's Name:	*Tana*
Baby's Name:	*Opal*
D.O.B.:	*12/10/87*
T.O.B.:	*daytime*
Sex:	*female*
Weight:	
BoSe:	*yes*
Navel:	*Iodine*
Hernia?:	*no*
Teeth:	*all four*
Heart & Lungs:	
Temperature:	
Weather:	*clear*
Problems / Comments:	

In 1987 we bought an adult female llama, Tana. We had heard that having an older producing female around would help our young females settle, or get pregnant. Apparently, this is a practice used with horses. Tammy, one of our first females, still was not pregnant. Besides, projections from our first farm plan were based on the assumption of three producing females. We still only had two. Our minds were set on three.

We got a good deal on Tana because Curt could trim her nails. She would not let her owner pick up her feet. For the price, we were guaranteed a female appaloosa baby. Half the money was paid up front, the other half was due upon the birth of the female cria. Tana was supposed to be due in early October. She did not deliver until December. We had bought a fat llama. Tana was expecting her fourth baby.

We were ecstatic when the baby finally arrived, a beautiful red appaloosa female. Again, we were not home when this one came. There were absolutely no problems. It is a joy to watch an experienced mother. No nonsense. The baby, Opal, was up and nursing by 4 o'clock when I got home. Iodine, BoSe, by this time we were doing enemas, too.

Enemas

When we first got into llamas, giving enemas was the thing to do. At first we used Fleets for infants. Crias got an enema right away, during those precious six hours when baby needs to be bonding and nursing. After a while somebody discovered warm water worked just as well, so everybody switched. Enema bottles were washed out and reused. Finally someone asked, "What are we doing this for? Llamas have existed for thousands of years without enemas."

Some smart person decided to wait for 24 hours before giving the enema. Somebody else decided to observe their crias to see what actually happens. Observation by breeders showed that crias do not need enemas during the first 24 hours and most crias do not need one at all.

If an infant is sluggish or straining, then it is reasonable to try an enema to see if it will help. Routine enemas are usually not required. Talk this procedure over with your vet to decide when and if it is necessary.

Parturition

Parturition is the veterinary term for birthing. I have avoided the word in my stories.

CHAPTER 3- 1988

April 29, 1988 Marvy Sue

Dam's Name:	*Mary*
Baby's Name:	*Marvy Sue*
D.O.B.:	*4/29/88*
T.O.B.:	*6 p.m.*
Sex:	*female*
Weight:	
BoSe:	*yes*
Navel:	*Iodine*
Hernia?:	*no*
Teeth:	*all four*
Heart & Lungs:	
Temperature:	
Weather:	*clear*
Problems / Comments:	

Curt had always wanted a white llama with a brown saddle. Marvy Sue fit the bill. Marvy was big, strong, active right from the start. We named her after radio and TV star Geoff Edwards' wife and sometimes radio DJ, Marvy Sue. You probably had to grow up in Los Angeles and listen to KMPC to get that one.

Marvy Sue's birth was uneventful except in human terms. I was at weaving class. Someone brought me a phone message. It said ,"Mary had a baby girl." I was beside myself. One of the ladies asked me if Mary was my daughter. I packed up my things and hurried home to see the baby. Curt had witnessed the blessed event.

Curt had already done the iodine and BoSe. I put the placenta in double plastic bags, labeled it and shoved it into the freezer. I'm not just sure what we thought we'd ever do with it, but we froze it nevertheless.

Up until now, our other babies had all been nursing by the time we found them. Marvy had not nursed yet. She was our first evening baby. We had Mary and Marvy confined to the barn with the lights on. Marvy explored every corner and shadow cribbing on all the surfaces. She was especially attracted to the corners. Up and down she explored everything but mom.

Finally, we changed the lighting and blocked off the corners with hay bales. By reducing the shadows, the baby became more interested in mom. We hung a light over Mary to make the shadow of her udder stronger. Marvy began cribbing on mom, nibbling on her wool. Eventually she got under and made a connection. It is easiest for baby to find mom's udder out in the open under the midday sun. While bringing mother and cria into the barn for observation makes life easier for the humans, it complicates things for the llamas.

Five babies and still no problems. Everything was going as promised. So far we had four girls and one boy. We thought we were pretty lucky.

LaRue Johnson's Neonatal Class

During the summer of 1988 I took one of LaRue Johnson's neonatal classes. I was determined to be prepared. It was in Central Oregon and all the big breeders were there. I felt as if I were the only little guy in the crowd. The hardest thing was learning how to deliver dead crias from artificial moms. Handling those dead babies was not easy. I've taught biology and have done plenty of dissections, but these were llamas. In my mind, that is close to being human. I learned more than I hoped I would ever need. I went home and upgraded my baby box. I also began a one woman campaign to persuade Dr. Brad Smith to do a Neonatal Clinic at OSU.

Meconium

Meconium is the first feces passed by a newborn. It can be quite dark and tarlike in consistency and can form a plug. Most crias manage to pass it without problems. You may miss it even with careful observation. A few may have problems. A cria seen straining over the dung pile needs an enema to help it along. After the meconium comes a white milky residue. It takes some time for a cria to start passing pellets.

The herd checks out a new cria.

September 8, 1988 Francis and the Yellow Jackets

Dam's Name:	*Gretchen*
Baby's Name:	*Francis*
D.O.B.:	*9/8/88*
T.O.B.:	*daytime*
Sex:	*female*
Weight:	
BoSe:	*yes*
Navel:	*Iodine*
Hernia?:	*no*
Teeth:	*all four*
Heart & Lungs:	
Temperature:	
Weather:	*sunny*
Problems / Comments:	*enema*

I saw Francis when I stopped to get the mail, a white spot on the green slope below our house. It's about a mile from the mailbox up the hill and back around to the house. I had to stop and unlock the gate on the way. When I finally got to the house, I leaped out of the car and charged around to the backyard gate. There it was, halfway down the hill towards the pond, lying in the afternoon sun. The cria was bright white in the sunshine. I ran to it. Boy or girl? Whatever it was, it had a black tail. I lifted the tail and looked. Girl! I picked her up, called for Gretchen and carried the baby into the barn.

Gretchen had passed her placenta under the shade of the walnut tree. By now I knew I needed to check it out to make sure it was whole with both horns. The placenta was covered with yellow jackets. I covered it with a water bucket, figuring I'd check it after dark when the yellow jackets had gone. I had other things to do. Curt would not be home right away and I had no way to reach him. This time it was my responsibility to take care of the newborn cria.

White babies look more frail than dark ones. Their

pink skin shows through their white hair until they dry off enough to fluff out. First the iodine. I hadn't really done this by myself before. Curt had always been there to hold. Francis squirmed all over the place. Eventually I had her navel dipped, but by then I had an orange baby, orange T-shirt, and bright orange hands. Iodine stung. It would not wash off.

Next came the shot. Somehow I did not understand that BoSe is just a shot, not a vaccination of any kind. It is just an injection of the trace mineral selenium to prevent White Muscle Disease. It is given in our area because our soil is deficient. It is usually given shortly after birth, but anytime in the first 24 hours or so is acceptable. I personally have never seen a case of White Muscle Disease. Chances are that whatever breeders in my area are doing, it is enough. However, at the time I believed that it was imperative that I give that shot right now. You can't just walk up to a cria and say, "Hold still while I stick you with this needle." Again, Curt and I had usually given shots as a team. He held, I stuck. I'm sure somebody has a better technique for giving a shot to an active baby all by yourself. After the iodine, Francis did not want anything to do with me. I ended up holding her between my legs while I pinched the back of her little bottom and gave the shot. I think she hated the alcohol swab more than the actual injection.

Finally I warmed the enema in a thermos of warm water. When it was lukewarm I caught baby between my legs again and inserted the enema bottle and squeezed. We were using regular baby enemas from the drug store. I waited a few minutes and sure enough something came out.

At dusk I went out to check the placenta. The bucket was just where I had left it. I lifted it up. The placenta was gone accept for a few small pieces. The yellow jackets had carried it off bit by bit.

Five girls to one boy. So far we were beating the odds. Mathematically we knew we had an even 50/50 chance of getting a boy or a girl. Girls were worth more money and they represented the only way we could hope to expand our herd. We were thankful to get our run of girls at the beginning.

IgG

IgG stands for immunoglobulin gamma, one of a family of proteins capable of acting as antibodies. In humans it is the principal immunoglobulin that moves across the placental barrier. In llamas it must come from colostrum. Perhaps because it is so well studied in humans that this is the immunoglobulin that we test for in llamas. Babies with low IgG levels can be transfused with plasma to build up the immune system. Some farms test all babies. Others test only those where there may be a question about sufficient colostrum intake.

White and wonderful cria in spring grass.

December 17, 1988 Dick: Cast

Dam's Name:	*Tana*
Baby's Name:	*Dick*
D.O.B.:	*12/17/88*
T.O.B.:	*about 7 a.m.*
Sex:	*male*
Weight:	
BoSe:	*yes*
Navel:	*Iodine*
Hernia?:	*no*
Teeth:	*o.k.*
Heart & Lungs:	*o.k.*
Temperature:	*o.k.*
Weather:	*cold*
Problems / Comments:	*could not stand Tubed*

Tana was expecting another December baby. We were hoping for early December, but that wasn't to be. December 17 was my parents' 50th wedding anniversary. We planned to take a day off work and drive to California for the celebration. We arranged to leave Tana at the vets' house for the impending birth. We would drop her and the trailer off in the morning on the way out of town. We would drive straight through to Atascadero and arrive in time for the party on Saturday. It would be about a 20 hour drive. So much for plans.

It was late. The car was packed for the anticipated morning departure. We were tired and getting ready for bed. The phone rang. Grandma was dead at 93. We were needed as soon as we could get there. There was no way to cancel the party because guests were already arriving from out of town. Mom was devastated.

First we had to hook up the new trailer. This is when we learned an important lesson. Always leave the trailer where it is instantly accessible by the least experienced driver. Curt had parked the trailer in the girls' pasture. I held the flashlight and directed Curt to back up. After about the tenth try, we managed to get things lined up and the trailer hitched to our 4 wheel drive Jimmy. Curt pulled the rig forward down the slope through the gate to the driveway. We had not counted on the frost. As he pulled through the gate, the entire rig slid sideways to the right, taking out the gate post. Neither the Jimmy nor our new trailer was damaged. However, the gatepost was jammed up against the hitch preventing forward or backward movement. The gate was wedged in there somewhere, too. We blocked everything in place to prevent the trailer from sliding over the bank and proceeded to work on extracting ourselves from our mess.

Next, we went out to catch Tana in the dark. Negotiating our hill by flashlight is no easy thing. The ground was covered with frost making walking on the grassy slope a real treat. Tana did not want to be caught. Chasing a full term llama around on a frozen hillside did not seem like a good thing. Eventually I bribed her with grain and coaxed her down to the barn.

Loading Tana into the trailer did not go as planned. Tana refused to get in. She threw her 400 pound plus body on the ground. She screamed. She spit. We tried a plywood ramp since she refused to step up. It sagged under her weight and she threw herself down again. Eventually we lifted, tugged and shoved her into the trailer on the plywood. We loaded in a couple bales of her familiar hay, wiped off the green slime, and drove out the driveway.

We pulled in the vet's yard at midnight. Although we had called earlier to say we were coming, we were so late he had long given up on us and went to bed. It was too late to put Tana out in the field, so we put her in a tiny stall in the barn. It was the only one available. She would be put into more appropriate quarters in the morning. We apologized to the vet and headed south.

A phone call awaited us 20 hours later when we arrived at my folks. Tana had given birth to a baby boy. The vet had checked her at six in the morning, as he left for morning rounds at the clinic. He returned at about eight to put her out in the pasture and found the cria. Tana had given birth in the tiny wooden stall. The stress of the previous night had been too much. The baby looked a little early and appeared a bit weak, not a real preemie, but he had concerns.

The next few days were hard. We had to face an anniversary party turned into a wake and make arrangements for a funeral in Los Angeles. Because of the weekend, the funeral could not be until Tuesday. A battle erupted with the cemetery over the plot. Luckily the Fireman's Relief Association stepped in and saved the day. Phone calls kept coming from the vet. The baby wouldn't stand. Tana had been milked out and the baby tubed. IgG levels had been checked and everything was acceptable. Still, the baby would not stand. He had to be held up to nurse. We were needed back ASAP.

Tuesday, right after the funeral, we pulled out of San Pedro and headed north into a driving rainstorm. Visibility was bad. Roads were flooded. At Redding rain turned into snow. Somewhere at the top of the Siskiyous we pulled into a rest stop exhausted. We could not go any further. We huddled in the back of the Jimmy and tried to get some sleep. Needless to say two six foot plus frames do not fit into the back of a Jimmy. We woke when it was too cold to sleep any longer. It was near white out conditions and we were all alone in the rest stop, no cars, no trucks, just us. We pulled out onto I-5. It was empty. Nothing. We headed north thinking we would get off at our first opportunity. Drifts were piled so high we could not get off the empty road. The road had been closed while we slept. We kept going north through the blowing snow. It was not safe to stop. It was the only way to go. Eventually we arrived at a road block at the top of the grade into Ashland. Trucks were jackknifed on both sides of the highway. We sat and waited, relieved to be near other people. A highway patrolman knocked on our window. Since we were 4 wheel drive, we had been selected to be the first vehicle down the mountain. About half way down the grade we watched the headlights of the car behind us fishtail off the road. We pulled into Ashland and had a huge breakfast at the bakery. We called the vet. He needed us now. Things were not going well. No time to sleep. We headed north.

Tana loves our vet. She is so good for him, never spits, lets him do all kinds of unspeakable things. However, she was glad to get home. Dick would nurse propped up against her leg. He was very reluctant to get up and down. He did not run like other babies. He could not negotiate our hill. Something was surely wrong, but what? He had passed all the blood tests. Heart and lungs were good. He was gaining weight.

Careful observation gave us the answer. X-rays at OSU confirmed it. Dick had broken one of the tiny bones in his foot.

We pieced together what might have happened. When Tana delivered in that tiny stall she probably turned around, hitting Dick's foot on a protruding corner stall board. The other possibility was that she stepped on him. It is likely that she would have done more damage if she had stepped on him. The injury would have been obvious from the start.

Llama babies are vulnerable when they first emerge front legs and nose first. A mom often tries to turn to see what is coming out. She may get up and down and even roll, all with baby sticking halfway out. It is not a good idea to confine mom at this point. Babies are better off born out in the field where mom has plenty of room. Also, open fields, especially grassy ones, are much cleaner than most barns where germs get concentrated. In Tana's case, the baby came much sooner than expected due to the stress. We were lucky she did not have him in the trailer while we were cruising down I-5 in the middle of the night.

What to do? The bone did not need to be set. It would heal, but Dick was in pain, sitting most of the time. He needed to be kept on level ground so he would not fall and injure it further. Stall rest was the recommendation. The leg needed to be splinted to make it easier for him to stand and nurse. However, after the first week or so the splint had to be rotated to the other leg every other day so that his legs would grow evenly. Curt made the splint out of PVC pipe cut in half and then trimmed to size. He lined it with fabric covered neoprene for padding. Velcro straps were glued on to hold it in place. Each day Dick's leg was padded and wrapped and covered with a clean child's tube sock with toe cut off. The splint was applied. Finally adhesive tape was used to keep it from slipping.

We put up a pen in the backyard made of four farm gates. On nice days we carried Dick, followed by Tana, outside to the pen for a little bit. This was winter. It was dark early and some days the weather was nasty. Tana became a real slime mother, she spit at us all the time. I had to wear a plastic raincoat, hat and goggles to go into the stall to work on Dick. With no reaction, she eventually gave it up.

Dick legs were so crooked we thought he might have angular limb deformity. When he was weaned we took him back to OSU and more x-rays. No, we were told. His growth plates looked fine. He would grow out of it. Sure enough by summer Dick looked and acted normal. He even won some ribbons.

Dick loved to ride in our VW van and we took him everywhere he was so much fun. We had him gelded at 18 months because we had been warned about berserk llamas. Eventually he was sold and went to live on another farm where he remained fun loving, friendly and well mannered to this day.

So much for the myth that llama babies are only born between 10 A.M.. and 2 P.M. Granted, this birth was complicated by stress.

CHAPTER 4 - 1989

1989 April 14, 1989 First OSU Neonatal Clinic

This was a birth of sorts. Curt and I attended the first Neonatal Clinic at OSU put on by Drs. Brad Smith and Pat Long. My determination paid off. Curt, having previously trained as an EMT in his LA County Lifeguard days, took the medical part to heart. More goodies went into the baby box. He built a wooden chute to help with exams.

This is Heather a few minutes after her birth. She was born in the barn while we were loading hay into the loft directly overhead.

August 28, 1989 Heather: At Last We Get to See One, Almost

Dam's Name:	*Gretchen*
Baby's Name:	*Heather*
D.O.B.:	*8/28/89*
T.O.B.:	*10:40 a.m.*
Sex:	*female*
Weight:	*31 lbs*
BoSe:	*yes*
Navel:	*Iodine*
Hernia?:	*no*
Teeth:	*all four*
Heart & Lungs:	*good °*
Temperature:	*100.9*
Weather:	*hot/clear*
Problems / Comments:	*enema*

Our barn can hold about six tons of hay in the loft if it is stacked carefully. We have an old hay elevator that will move one bale at a time. This is fine with me because my job is to stack the hay. It is slow enough that I can keep up with it. We usually haul our own hay. It makes for a long, hot, tiring day. The llama girls love to snack on the new hay as we unload it. We keep the area under the hay elevator blocked off for safety. Occasionally a bale falls off. We do not want to hit a llama. Also, we do not want a llama tripping on the electrical cord.

Our female herd is up to nine, four purchased adults and five home grown young females. I have yet to see one of my own babies be born. Gretchen is pushing and shoving for the new hay like everyone else. I do not think she will deliver for a few more days. She is just too active. A bale breaks and falls off the elevator. I climb down the ladder and clean up the mess, tossing the hay into the manger inside the barn. Some of the girls go around to the other door to get to the manger. Gretchen goes in the barn. I can not see her from the loft because she is directly below me. Occasionally I catch a glimpse of her nose in the manger. Curt can not see into the barn from the trailer because the door is shut on his side.

Finally the trailer is empty. We need to go pick up one more load, but first an ice tea break. I come down the ladder. Curt comes in the door. Gretchen is standing at the manger eating new hay. A brown and white cria is laying at her feet. We missed it. We were right there and did not see Heather's birth. Gretchen still has to pass her placenta. I rush into the house to get the baby box. I get the BoSe shot out of the refrigerator. I tuck the syringe into my pocket to warm it up to body temperature. We've given up on Fleets. I take a clean used enema bottle and fill it with warm water. Grabbing the camera and dry towels, I return to the barn. Little wet Heather was struggling to stand on shaky legs.

The baby box now includes a small notebook where all important information gets recorded: date, time of birth, sex, baby's temperature, pulse, respirations, heart and lung sounds, nursing, urination, bowel movements. Amazing what a little class can do.

Young llama baby greets the newest cria.

September 28, 1989 Yvonne: False Security

Dam's Name:	*Mary*
Baby's Name:	*Yvonne*
D.O.B.:	*9/28/89*
T.O.B.:	*daytime*
Sex:	*female*
Weight:	*27.5 lbs*
BoSe:	*yes*
Navel:	*Iodine*
Hernia?:	*no*
Teeth:	*not fully erupted*
Heart & Lungs:	*good*
Temperature:	*102.9*
Weather:	*warm/clear*
Problems / Comments:	*monitor temp*

During the summer of 1989 Curt's parents arrived on our doorstep. They had lost their job as caretakers of a major Palm Springs estate. Failing health had caught up with them. This time they were to retire for good. We were to enter a new phase of our lives, dealing with declining parents. We have a large house, so making room was no problem. Curt's hope was that they would take an interest in the llamas. Having someone at home during the day was a plus. We had them watch the llama birthing video over and over again.

September came and we were back to work. State Fair was behind us but we still had one more big livestock show to go, during the last weekend of the month. A week before the fair we blew the engine on our Volkswagen Vanagon. The morning of the fair, as Curt went to hook up the trailer, the differential went out on the Jimmy. That left us with our 63 VW Crewcab. We lashed down our gear in the pickup bed, took out the back seat, and proceeded to load two llamas in the back of the cab. Leaving Bob and Fran to watch Mary, we drove the 50 miles to the fair.

During the day we called twice. "Yes, Mary is doing just fine. No baby."

The fair closed at 5 o'clock. Curt went to get the crewcab to load the llamas. A crowd gathered to watch us put the two males into the back seat area. Pulling out of the fairgrounds, the clutch went out. No freeway for us. We would have to return home by backroads. The VW would not go over 30 miles an hour. It was a trick to get it to start up, too. It was a beautiful fall day winding through the Oregon countryside. Leaves were just beginning to turn orange against the green grassy hillsides. We'd lost three cars in one week, but everything would be okay. Bob and Fran were at home watching the farm. We would be home in time for a late dinner and then we could do chores.

We limped up the driveway. Bob would have to take us to work the next morning. We could get the Jimmy fixed. The Vanagon would have to be sold as is for its body. The crewcab went into the garage where it stayed for the next six years. That is how long it took for Curt to ever have spare time again. Fran had dinner waiting. It was great to know things were under control and all was right with the farm.

We went out to the barn to do evening chores and feed the llamas at 7:00 P.M. I called the girls. Here comes Mary, a little white cria by her side. This baby had been out for some time. It was all dry and fluffy, a carbon copy of mom. We lifted the tail, a girl. Curt went for the baby box and I went to look for the placenta. I found it under the shade of a fir tree. I almost missed it in the fading evening light. I inspected it. The placenta was cold, but whole. This confirmed my suspicions that the baby had been born hours before. I wrapped the placenta up for the freezer.

Back in the barn, I held the baby while Curt checked it over. The edges of four teeth were not fully erupted. Heart and lung sounds were good. Pulse was 108. Ears were long and erect. She weighed 27 1/2 pounds. Temperature was a little high, 102.9°. Our target is 99° to 102°. We called the vet. We gave

31

a BoSe shot and iodine, but skipped the enema. At 8 P.M. we saw her nurse. At 11 P.M. we saw a bowel movement, probably not her first. The vet called back. We were to give 1 cc penicillin for 5 days and check temperature twice a day. Call if the temperature stayed above 103°.

Fall progressed. Yvonne grew into a big, happy baby. Fran and Bob could not stand the rain. They returned to the desert and Fran's familiar dialysis clinic. The llamas never did interest them like they do us.

White and elegant female cria.

Injections

Have your vet teach you how to give injections. I had to learn to give shots to myself since I am allergic to bee stings. You need to know the difference between subQ and IM and the various injection sites. Clare Hoffman's book Caring for Llamas and Alpacas covers giving injections. Be careful. I recently had a llama kick and I accidentally vaccinated myself.

Curt is giving this newborn cria a BoSe injection.

December 5, 1989 Sheila: Early Morning Blues

Dam's Name:	*Tana*
Baby's Name:	*Sheila*
D.O.B.:	*12/5/89*
T.O.B.:	*7 a.m.*
Sex:	*female*
Weight:	*30 lbs*
BoSe:	*yes*
Navel:	*iodine*
Hernia?:	*no*
Teeth:	*yes*
Heart & Lungs:	*good*
Temperature:	*99.3°*
Weather:	*32° frost, fog*
Problems / Comments:	

I am wakened by an alarm call. It is four in the morning. I pull on some sweat pants under my night gown, wrap myself into a heavy coat, cover my head with a home spun llama wool hat, grab a flashlight, put on my boots and head out the door. Something is wrong. The gates are open, not just one gate, but every gate on the place is wide open. The three studs are screaming, running at high speed through the girls' pasture. The girls are all in the highest corner, formed into a circle facing out. Tana is in the middle. I check her out. She looks fine. I begin the task of closing gates and catching boys. My neighbor's son, a Viet Nam Vet, the one who blew up the signal at our local rural intersection, must be home from the state hospital again. I'm back in bed at five.

Six o'clock. I wrap up again and go out to check on Tana. I'm concerned about the early morning stress. I want to check on her before Curt leaves for work. She's fine. I wave good bye to Curt from the pasture.

Time to go to work. It is 7:30 A.M. Dressed for work, I head out to check one last time. There she is, in the highest corner, white cria by her side. The grass is much slicker than it had been earlier. A thick early morning fog had crept up the valley and clung to the hillside. Ice was forming where it touched the ground. I inched my way up the hill. My work shoes were no match for the frost. I felt like the frog in the well, two steps forward, one step back. About the time I get to the top, Tana slimed me from head to toe. She won't let me near her baby. I can't pick it up anyway because I can not maneuver down the hill. I work my way over to the field fence and steady myself down the slope. I walk back to the house and call work. I will not be there this morning. I'll see them at noon.

I change into my farmer clothes and fill my pockets with a film can full of iodine, a syringe of BoSe, a thermometer and some dry towels. I put on my special plastic raincoat, goggles and hat. I put boots on for better traction and head back up the hill. I still can not make it to the baby. After our early morning activities Tana is really stressed. She won't let me near. I finally give up. I go back to the house and call Curt at work. I tell him that Tana had her baby but, she won't let me near it. He'll have to arrange for someone to cover his classes. He's coming home. It might be more than an hour before he arrives. I go back outside.

This time I crawl up the hill. Tana spits at me but she does not try to stomp me or body block me. I reach the baby. Gathering it up in my arms and standing up, the real trouble begins. Tana is pushing me. She has four foot drive and her toe nails dig into the mud and frozen ground. I just slide. I hang on and pray we do not get hurt. I still do not know if the baby is a boy or girl.

Eventually we make it back down the hill to the barn. I'm exhausted. I sit down and start rubbing the baby with a towel. This one will need the hair dryer. Tana passes her placenta. Baby gets up and noses mom. By 8:12 A.M. she has nursed all four teats. Curt arrives. Tana calms down once baby nursed. Together we check vitals, dip the navel, and finish drying her off. Her temperature is 99.3°, not bad for a cold, frosty

Llama Babies

morning. By 9:50 A.M. we see first poop. No enema
for this one. Last thing before leaving the barn, we
put a cria blanket on the baby. Since it is cold today,
we will leave mother and baby in the barn. I showered and dress for work for a second time in the day.

Because of the cold wet winter weather, we keep
Tana and Sheila in the barn each night. That saves
me from having to climb the hill by flashlight to check
on them during the night.

New crias are born wet and must dry off quickly.

Finding the Right Veterinarian

The time to find the right veterinarian is before there is a crisis. When we purchased our first llamas, we had a wonderful veterinarian for our dogs and cats. His practice included mostly dogs and horses with cats and general farm animals thrown in. While he was willing to provide emergency care for our animals, he was not interested in dealing with internal medicine for llamas. He was already overextended in horses. We asked him if there was anyone he would recommend. We called the Vet School and our extension office and asked for referrals. We asked the breeders from whom we had purchased our llamas who they used. We asked all our llama neighbors.

Two names appeared on almost every list. One clinic served the north end of the valley and the other served the south. We were right in the overlap. Because we are south of town, it is easier for us to travel south to the vet's than to drive north through town. We started with south, but we tried both. Curt soon became good friends with the doctor we selected.

Where we live in Salem, we have access to four veterinarians with years of llama experience plus the School of Veterinary Medicine. We could not ask for better access. However, we still have experienced our vet and two back up vets all being out of town to the same llama conference. A farm can never have enough back up vets. Disasters always happen when the vet is on vacation.

Several criteria make up the list of qualifications for a good llama vet. High on my list of importance is, does this person's style mesh with mine? Do we communicate well? Can we function as a team? Availability is another big item. When is the vet available for farm calls? Can I bring a llama to the clinic? What happens after hours? Is someone on call? Can I call in the middle of the night? Llamas need care 24 hours a day. Interest in learning more about llamas is important. Affordable services may be an issue as well as method of payment. Experience with llamas is a plus, but curiosity and willingness to learn are more important. Taking an active roll in the local llama community is important to me.

Younger vets have had more training with llamas while in school than older vets did even ten years ago. Today llamas are included in the regular curriculum of study in most vet schools. If an experienced llama vet is not available, look for a junior partner who may have an interest in developing a llama practice.

Many veterinarians do not have surgery facilities for large animals. This is the case with our primary vet. Lucky for us, we are close to the vet school. However, the vet school is expensive. All surgical procedures are done in a state of the arts operating room. There are times we need a less expensive alternative. We located a clinic with large animal x-ray and surgical facilities that we use for less serious situations.

Part of finding the right veterinarian is learning how to be a good client. Good veterinary service is a team effort. Schedule routine appointments in advance. Be clear about what you want done during the visit. Be ready when the vet arrives. Have the llamas caught up in advance. Provide a safe environment for the vet to work in. A chute is nice and a must if you have several animals. Good lighting is important. Hot water and clean towels might be appreciated. Desensitize and train your animals. A vet visit should not turn into a rodeo. Write down instructions and follow them out. Discuss your concerns calmly. Share your criteria for decision making. Accept responsibility for your herd management practices. Call the vet in time. A llama does not look sick until it is almost too late to save it. Do not waste time. Do not blame failures on the vet. Always pay your bills on time. Be as open and honest as you can. This is an important relationship worthy of putting large amounts of energy into maintaining it.

Learn to accommodate other farm's emergencies that may call the vet away from his scheduled appointments. Be flexible. You never know when you may be the one with a problem birth or sick llama. Learn to take your animal's vital signs so that you can give them over the phone. Try to be accurate in your observations. Good information helps the vet evaluate the situation and determine a course of action.

Wormings, vaccinations, geldings, fighting teeth removal, and pregnancy testing are the kinds of routine procedures to use to get to know a new veterinarian. If you do not like the person doing ordinary things, it is not likely you will like that person when your favorite llama is dying. Don't wait for a disaster to try to find the right vet.

Maggie and cria.

CHAPTER 5- 1990

Barbara drying off cria in the kitchen.

March 18, 1990 Steve: Good Morning

Dam's Name:	*Alice*
Baby's Name:	*Steve*
D.O.B.:	*3/18/90*
T.O.B.:	*before 7:00 a.m.*
Sex:	*male*
Weight:	*24.75 lbs*
BoSe:	*yes*
Navel:	*Iodine*
Hernia?:	*no*
Teeth:	*yes*
Heart & Lungs:	*good*
Temperature:	*97°*
Weather:	*mild/wet*
Problems / Comments:	*dried and jacket*

It was not a work day, so we sleep in. We don't get to do that very often at our house. We had a hot breakfast together, then Curt went out to check on the girls. We were expecting two spring babies. Both first time moms were born on our farm. Somehow this makes us feel more like real llama breeders. Curt runs back into the house. Alice had her baby! It's a boy. We grab the baby box and head for the barn.

Steve had been out for a while. It is 8:30 A.M. He is already nursing. Crias often do not nurse until after the placenta has passed. In our experience it takes about an hour after birth for mom to pass her placenta. It is a normal wet Oregon morning. The baby is not dry yet. Curt takes some towels and the hair dryer and proceeds to dry him off. I take a bucket and go out hunting for the placenta. When I find the placenta, it is already cold. Placentas can retain their heat for an hour or two. That makes the baby at least two or three hours old.

Back in the barn, Curt has finished with the Iodine and BoSe. The baby weighs 24 3/4 pounds, a little light for us. Vitals are all good except his temperature is 97°. On goes the cria jacket. I put down a

41

layer of dry clean straw for baby to cush in. By 10:00 A.M. his temperature is 99.2°.

Steve's birth was unassisted and normal, but it did not take place between 10 A.M. and 2 P.M.

At six months of age, on a Sunday morning, Steve broke his leg. He and Alice were playing chase in our front pasture, frolicking around doing pirouettes. Curt and I were working outside when Alice brought Steve up the hill to Curt. Steve was walking on three legs, his left front leg dangling limp. Alice followed Curt into the barn. She obviously expected him to make it better right now.. Steve was stoic and brave. I ran to the house to get supplies to splint the leg with. Curt checked for lacerations. Curt sorted through the collection of potential splints, padding and bandages. I think we finally used magazines (straight out of Red Cross First Aid). We needed to immobilize the joints. We called the vet. Steve would have to go to OSU. Prognosis was not good. Nobody had done many llama legs. We picked him up and loaded him into the van. We called OSU and told them we were coming.

Steve had a spiral fracture. He had probably come down in a gopher hole and twisted. His leg would need to be pinned. That required surgery. The cast would be on for at least six weeks. There might need to be an additional surgery to reset the pins. Also, the cast would need to be changed every two to three weeks. The leg would need to be x-rayed several times during the process. OSU suggested that Steve stay at the vet school the whole time. We chose to take him home and bring him in as needed, partly because of the expense and partly because llamas do better at home. Steve did have to stay at the vet school for about a week. Since Steve was not weaned, the week was even more stressful. Curt and I went to see him every evening after work.

Steve was a wonderful patient. He hobbled around on three legs, never damaging the cast. He was good about his shots. He never complained about stall rest. His one big disappointment came when he got home. Alice, his mom, would not have a thing to do with him. He was weaned and that was that. Everyone at OSU was amazed at how fast and how well Steve healed. Curt carted him back and forth once a week for six weeks. He needed one more surgery to remove the pins. He had to wear a splint for a week or so while the leg strengthened up. We traded a Komondor pup for a slightly younger male llama so he would have a companion during his recuperation. We kept Steve until he was about 30 months old before he was sold with full disclosure. He still is an active herdsire.

Steve made two personal appearances with the OSU staff and his x-rays. One was at a presentation for a large group of veterinarians. The other was at the WVLA/OSU Annual Herd Health Day. The veterinarians could not even find the scar from the pins nor could they tell which leg had been broken.

Brown mom, appy baby, and friend.

March 30, 1990 Alma

Dam's Name:	*Irene*
Baby's Name:	*alma*
D.O.B.:	*3/30/90*
T.O.B.:	*daytime*
Sex:	*female*
Weight:	*28 lbs*
BoSe:	*yes*
Navel:	*Iodine*
Hernia?:	*no*
Teeth:	*all four*
Heart & Lungs:	*good*
Temperature:	*101.7°*
Weather:	*mild*
Problems / Comments:	

Alma, Irene's first baby came without problems. Irene is very athletic. She never slows down. She ran and played with the youngsters in the evening up to the day she had her baby. Alma came during the day while we were at work. We found her dry and nursing when we got home. It was a nice warm spring day. Our girls usually know how to pick the good weather.

Curt predicts birthing days by looking at my tentative dates and the long term weather forecast. If it is raining six out of the next seven days, he says the baby will come on the one sunny day. He is usually right.

Ordinarily we start baby watch two weeks before the due date. I get up and check the girls before Curt leaves. I've learned the hard way that I may need help. It's easier to get him before he leaves for work. One of us, usually me, comes directly home from work as soon as possible. If I am going to be late, I call Curt and he comes home. Curt only hurries home if it is warm and sunny.

We were surprised to see that two dark brown parents had produced an appy baby. We had expected dark brown. Alma was white with lots of black spots. We were still doing good on our male/female ratio, three males to nine females.

Dystocia

Dystocia is a fancy word that means problem delivery. Do not expect to learn how to deal with dystocia from a book. This is one of those things, like swimming, you must learn from experience. Take a Neonatal Clinic. Check with your local Veterinary Teaching Hospital. Clinics are often offered as part of a conference. Your local llama association may arrange to put one on. Clinics are not cheap because they need specialized equipment as well as a competent presenter. If you plan to be a llama breeder, a Neonatal Clinic is the best investment of your time and money you can possibly make.

Nose to nose.

April 7, 1990 Tammy's C-Section

Tammy was one of our original three weanling pairs. By five years old, she had never gotten pregnant. She had all her parts and seemed to be hormonally balanced. She had every test known to our vet. She had a fairly nasty uterus infection which had required daily vaginal flushing and twice a day shots. I did not even have to halter her to give her a shot. I'd just say, "Tammy, time for your shot." She would just stand there for me. I did have to put her in the chute for her vaginal flushes. I was ready to give up, but the vet wasn't. We made a deal. He could take her home to provide her daily care, we'd split the baby. Luckily, a science teacher from my school lived next door to the vet. Tammy would board in her back pasture.

After several more tries, Tammy got pregnant. I would not bring her home. I wanted her right there at the vet's. She was due in May. I got daily reports on her from my friend. I visited her regularly. I got a weekly progress report from the vet.

On April 7th, Curt took me to Corvallis. I needed to pick up a book on poisonous plants I had ordered at the OSU bookstore. Then we were planning to pick up some pictures I had framed at a local art gallery. In the middle of all this I started to worry about Tammy. It was like a compulsion. I was sure something was wrong. I insisted that Curt take me to see Tammy right now.

As we pulled into his driveway, the vet was running out of the barn, blood dripping down both arms. It was like he was expecting us. "Scrub up," he said, "We are going to do a C-section." I knew I was not going to be much help because I was just recovering from major surgery and could barely move. I went next door and got my fellow teacher. She had done enough dissections to not be bothered by what we were about to do. The vet started to scold me. This was not going to be pretty and the baby would most likely be dead. My friend let him know she'd done just fine in anatomy class, besides, he really did need the help. We all went to work.

A barn is not a sterile environment. It is no place for major surgery. Tammy was already down, so location had been decided for us. It was too late to get her to OSU. While the vet was getting his tools together, we removed all the bedding from the ground. I think we sprayed the floor with something to keep down the dust, and covered the floor with sheets. We ushered the other llamas outside. Curt moved the lights so we could see.

I held the head, my friend held the feet. The vet cut and probed while Curt served as scrub nurse, monitored vitals and gave various injections. Tammy had gone into labor but her cervix did not open wide enough to let the baby through. Either she or the baby had bled considerably. We were in danger of loosing them both. We were not in time to save the baby. Curt laid it aside for future examination. It was a beautiful little black female, 24 pounds, big enough that she might have made it if she had not been compromised. The placenta would not detach. What to do? The vet debated with himself. He could not leave the placenta because it would never pass through the damaged cervix. It had been exposed to the outside environment so it would rot if he left it. That would surely kill Tammy. He started cleaning it out as best he could. Once the baby was out, the uterus started to collapse. The incision was just big enough to get the baby out. Placental fluids were causing a problem, They started to leak into her body cavity. Time was running out. He began the long job of sewing her back up.

I was exhausted. I knew the vet had worked all day before this started. Layer by layer he stitched. Curt finished closing up the external stitches. Together they bound her up. We rolled her up in a cush position and propped her up with hay bales. We began to clean up the mess. The vet mumbled something about keeping the sheets. I told him I would bring him a stack of fresh ones in the morning. I threw the soiled sheets into the trash. It was too early to tell if Tammy would make it. The vet went in to get some sleep. Curt and I went with my friend next door to her house to shower, clean up and eat Chinese takeout. We checked on Tammy before we went home. She was awake enough to stand. We moved her to a stall. I told her how sorry I was for the way things had turned out. I told her I would bring her home soon.

I never tried to breed Tammy after that. I'm sure she has had a few opportunities on her own, but we never had a Tammy baby. Three or four people have offered to buy her because she is so good with weanlings. I tell them she is not for sale.

The herd surrounds a new cria.

August 25,1990 Betty Chasing Momma on the Hill

Dam's Name:	*Opal*
Baby's Name:	*Betty*
D.O.B.:	*8/25/90*
T.O.B.:	*1:45 p.m.*
Sex:	*female*
Weight:	*24.5 lbs*
BoSe:	*yes*
Navel:	*Iodine*
Hernia?:	*no*
Teeth:	*all four*
Heart & Lungs:	*good*
Temperature:	*99.2°*
Weather:	*sunny/cumulus clouds*
Problems / Comments:	

Opal was expecting her first baby in late August, just before we were to go back to work and right before State Fair. August is hot in the Willamette Valley, not hot like other parts of the country, but maybe 80's and 90's, beautiful summer days. Because we are not far from the river, cool air moves up the valley every evening. It usually cools off at night. We breed from March to October, not skipping the summer months. We have lots of shade and put out sprinklers during the hottest days.

Curt and I were working outside on one of our many summer projects. With full time jobs, we try to get all the major construction and repairs done during July and August. The girls are in the lower pasture, enjoying the warm sun. Suddenly Curt sees a nose sticking out of Opal. No feet, just a nose. He calls me to look. Sure enough, just a nose. In a normal presentation, the feet appear first, and then the nose. This could be trouble, a first time mom and no feet showing. We put down our tools. We hurry in the house to get the baby box and call the vet.

Give it 15 minutes. In the mean time, get ready

49

to scrub up. Up until now, all our babies born on the farm had come out unassisted. We had helped with some other people's babies, but none of our own. We'd both attended the OSU Neonatal Clinic. We were prepared. Whatever was going to happen would be long over by the time the vet could get here. We grabbed the baby box, a halter, and lead.

Our first task was to catch Opal. That should be simple enough. She is a grain hog. Rattling the grain bucket would normally get her into the barn, but today was not just any day. She would not come. We tried herding her into the barn. She would have none of it. She raced around the pasture, just out of reach. She neatly avoided capture every time we thought we had her. She refused to be caught. By now the head was out completely. About the fourth time up and down the hill we saw a foot. Still, that other leg could be caught up just about anywhere.

You can not assist a birthing mom you can't catch, or can you? Opal continued to bounce up and down the hill. Curt was determined to catch her and she was determined to evade him. Pop! Out plopped the other foot. We now had a normal presentation. All that bouncing around had shook the baby's feet clear of the birth canal.

We sat down to rest. Mom proceeded to have a normal delivery. The baby was on the ground by 1:45 P.M. The placenta passed at 3:00 P.M. The cria, Betty, was a beautiful appaloosa girl with black and red spots. She nursed right away. We took lots of pictures.

One weird thing did happen. Tana, Opal's dam, was watching with the rest of the girls. When the baby started to squirm on the ground, Tana ran up spitting. She tried to stomp little Betty helplessly wiggling on the ground. I had to body block Tana to get her away. I put her in another pasture for about a month.

In retrospect what did I learn from watching this birth from start to finish? If you can't catch her, she probably doesn't need your help.

Placenta

The placenta is the large organ or sack that lines the uterus and contains the developing fetus. Llama placentas are different than those of humans. The attachment is different, being diffuse. More layers separate the fetus from the mother, making colostrum vital to pass on immunity. The placenta entirely fills both horns of the uterus even though the fetus is usually carried in the left horn.

The placenta is delivered after the cria. Similar to humans, this is called the third stage of labor. It is not unusual for this to occur up to 6 hours after birthing. In my experience 1 to 2 hours is more usual. Never pull on any placental tissue.

When the placenta has passed, spread it out and check to see if it is all there. If any large pieces are missing, call the vet. It is a good idea to wear gloves when handling placentas.

We keep the placenta for emergency use. I put it in a doubled kitchen sized garbage bag, tie it off, label it and put it in a small cardboard box in the freezer. I throw the old ones out when I need more space in the freezer.

We never have had to use a placenta. The purpose of keeping it is insurance in case mother and cria have to be separated for some reason. To assist the dam in recognizing and accepting her baby, the placenta is rubbed on the cria when it is reintroduced. If a cria is to be grafted onto another mother, the stored placenta of the foster mom can be used to encourage her to accept the strange baby.

September 21, 1990 Carol: Dry and Nursing

Dam's Name:	Mary
Baby's Name:	Carol
D.O.B.:	9/21/90
T.O.B.:	daytime
Sex:	female
Weight:	29 lbs.
BoSe:	yes
Navel:	Iodine
Hernia?:	no
Teeth:	all four
Heart & Lungs:	good
Temperature:	99.6°
Weather:	87° sunny, dry
Problems / Comments:	

Carol was Mary's fourth baby. She was born while we were at work. We found her at 3:20 P.M. dry and nursing. She weighed 29 pounds. I do not remember finding the placenta. The dogs probably ate it. She was our 15th baby. We were still way ahead on the girls. So far we had 11 girls and 3 boys, and one loss.

We felt especially blessed. It had taken so long for us to get started. At the time, prices were still high for females. We were able to sell some females to recover our investment. We kept some to expand our herd. We sold three females at the first Firecracker Sale for very good prices.

Selling your babies at auction to strangers is difficult. In fact it was so stressful for me that I passed out when the third one sold. My sister had to take me home and put me to bed. 1990 proved to be the only year I made more money from llamas than I did from teaching.

Choosing which llama to sell and which to keep is no easy thing. We tried to keep one female from each of our three adult females and sell one from each. We have never had problems selling our males. Curt has such a good time with them that people are always asking to buy them at fairs and events.

This newborn cria holds her neck in a typical curved position.

December 2, 1990 Chuck: Milk Fever

Dam's Name:	*Gretchen*
Baby's Name:	*Chuck*
D.O.B.:	*12/2/90*
T.O.B.:	*11:30 a.m.*
Sex:	*male*
Weight:	*26 lbs.*
BoSe:	*yes*
Navel:	*Iodine*
Hernia?:	*no*
Teeth:	*all four*
Heart & Lungs:	*good*
Temperature:	*101.3°*
Weather:	*fair*
Problems / Comments:	

Chuck was Gretchen's fifth baby. Gretchen had not bred back right away after her fourth baby, so Chuck was born late in the year. We had done all right with winter babies so far, but Chuck was to be the one to sour us on any more December babies. We are actually home more in December than any other month during the school year, but December has two things against it, three really. First, there is very little daylight in December. We go to work in the dark and come home in the dark. Second is the weather. It is cold and the winter of 90-91 was the coldest on record. We had minus 12 degree temperatures. The third issue is more social or family oriented. Our families always want us to come visit at Christmas.

Chuck was born at 11:30 in the morning on the first weekend in December. There were no problems. We were excited to have a boy. This one would be just the right age for fair season. We dried him off with the hair dryer and put him in a cria coat. Gretchen is such a good mom. Chuck was gaining a pound and a half a day, however Gretchen started losing weight. Just a little at first. We fed her extra, that had worked with her last baby. Twice a day, not just in the evening like the others. It meant I had to get up a half hour earlier to get her into the barn before daylight. Also, we decided not to rebred her until spring.

We always do herd health during Christmas Vacation. The vet arrived. I had all the girls in the barn except Gretchen. Chuck had come down with the others. While Curt and the vet got started, I walked up the hill to get Gretchen. I knew she would walk down with me to get her breakfast. Gretchen was cushed in the middle of the upper driveway. She could not get up. I checked her over. No visible broken legs or open wounds. She was almost unconscious. I ran back to the barn to get help. The men were slow to respond. What I was saying was so unexpected. Curt said he would go up and get her and walk her down. I went for my van.

We do not use the upper driveway in the winter anymore because it is so dangerous. In fact now it is blocked off. I carefully backed the van up the treacherous slope into the upper pasture. I pulled up beside Gretchen. Curt and the Vet had not been able to get her up. I opened the big door. The three of us picked her up and loaded her in like a sack of potatoes. Curt drove back down to the barn. We carried Gretchen in to be examined. Through a process of elimination, the vet decided Gretchen had Milk Fever, the calcium had suddenly dropped out of her blood. He took blood tests to be sure, but he immediately gave her an IV of calcium solution. Gretchen perked up right away, just like the cows in James Herriot's stories. We would need to keep her in at night where it was not quite as cold. We were to feed her alfalfa and calcium supplement. He left us with two large bottles of injectable calcium to use in case of emergency.

Gretchen continued to loose weight in spite of our efforts. We tried Tums, she liked the cherry ones. We tried every kind of supplemental feed. I forced vitamins in applesauce into her mouth when she would not eat it. I mixed bone meal with molasses and poured it on her feed. We encouraged the baby to eat. He continued to grow like a weed and Gretchen continued to decline.

In mid January temperatures fell to below zero. For the first time, I even had to bring my males inside the barn. They were too cold to fight. We piled up straw bales to keep out the wind. I had to carry warm water from the house. Our pipes froze. The electricity went out. Lucky for me, I had anticipated the power outage and had filled 10-12 five gallon buckets with water and stacked them in the downstairs bathroom. When the stored water ran out, I had to melt snow on the wood stove to have drinking water for the llamas.

The cold sapped the last energy out of Gretchen. She went down again. Curt gave the injectable calcium as instructed. This time she did not respond. We hauled her to OSU. They had never heard of milk fever in a llama. She was put on IV's and checked over for secondary problems. She would not eat at the vet school. Curt went down every night after work and fed her by hand. After a week we were told she was not responding to treatment. There was nothing else to do. We brought her home. Every evening I would come home dreading the thought of finding her dead in the barn. We hand fed her for weeks. Slowly she recovered.

Meanwhile, back at the farm, we had a six week old baby with no mom. We tried bottle feeding, but he refused. He was too big and active to tube. We were afraid he would starve. Lucky for him he was a big baby. After a few days we gave up on trying to force the bottle. He lost a few pounds but quickly began to eat Calf Manna. We set up a special creep feeder with alfalfa, llama pellets and Calf Manna. We made the door to the creep feeder too narrow and small for the other young llamas. At first we put him in it. He figured out how to get out. Soon he was going in and out. We widened the door as he grew.

Gretchen and Chuck were kept apart where they could not see each other. Chuck spent most of the time with his big sister Heather or Betty who was nine months older than him. Betty would even let him nurse. When Evan was born in June, Chuck was his faithful big brother. Eventually he had to move into the little boys' pasture with Steve and Buddy.

After Chuck, we decided that we did not have the reserves to deal with winter babies. Chuck is a good example of how winter weather can stretch a farm's ability to cope to the limits. This was a case of a normal, uneventful birth turning into a winter nightmare.

We would not have made it through had we not been able to hire Eric Thompson, a college student and former middle school student of Curt's to help out. Eric knew his way around cattle. He was strong, hard working and willing to learn and most important, the llamas liked him.

New crias often hold their necks in a distinctive S curve because the muscles in the back of the neck are stronger than those in the front. It takes work to pull the head forward.

CHAPTER 6- 1991

March 18, 1991 Diane

Dam's Name:	*Irene*
Baby's Name:	*Diane*
D.O.B.:	*3/18/91*
T.O.B.:	*12 noon*
Sex:	*female*
Weight:	*29 lbs.*
BoSe:	*yes*
Navel:	*Iodine*
Hernia?:	*no*
Teeth:	*all four*
Heart & Lungs:	*good*
Temperature:	*100.6°*
Weather:	*clear*
Problems / Comments:	

Spring break comes in March in Oregon. It has nothing to do with Easter. It used to have something to do with state basketball finals, but not anymore. The weather is unpredictable, often rainy. This time, however the weather was fair. We were working on spring cleaning around the farm and fence repair. At noon we came back up to the house.

The girls were all clustered at the back fence, watching something in the yard. Irene was looking over the fence humming. Her eyes were wide, white showing around brown. A brown and white paint cria was sitting in the yard. How did the baby get on the wrong side of the fence? I looked around. She had slipped under the barn door and tumbled down the steps to the yard. I checked her over, picked her up and carried her back into the barn. Irene met me at the door. I put the baby under mom. Diane, unharmed by her tumble, nursed right away.

To avoid a repeat accident, we moved the fencing so the barn would be entirely inside the pasture

59

fence. We had to give up about half the backyard and all my garden space.

Fencing Accidents

Fencing is a hazard for newborns. Examine your fences from the point of view of a little guy fresh in the world on wobbly legs. All fencing has its own potential for accidents and death. Fences on slopes are the biggest problem. A cria can tumble into it, head over heals and get trapped. Slipping under a fence is a problem. Ask breeders in your area what they have done to minimize fence injuries.

Fences are also a hazard to llamas being weaned. Youngsters will try to climb over, under and through fences, sometimes with disastrous results. Be proactive about preventing accidents.

Lunch time.

April 13, 1991 Eileen: Heart Murmur Found

Dam's Name:	Alice
Baby's Name:	Eileen
D.O.B.:	4/13/91
T.O.B.:	early morning
Sex:	female
Weight:	28 lbs.
BoSe:	yes
Navel:	Iodine
Hernia?:	no
Teeth:	all four
Heart & Lungs:	whoosh sound
Temperature:	99.4°
Weather:	clear
Problems / Comments:	heart murmur

I found Alice's baby on one of my early morning trips out into the pasture to check on the girls. I was not exactly sure of Alice's due date, but according to my best guess it was soon. I was into my baby watch mode. I reminded Curt not to leave without checking with me. Dressed in my nightgown, overcoat, boots, and knit llama wool hat I went first to the barn before climbing the hill. The girls usually do not sleep in the barn. They bed down out in the pasture. They come in if it is raining hard. They usually come back down to the barn in the morning to eat breakfast. Only a few early birds were in the barn. I could see Alice outside the big double doors. Good. I did not need to climb the hill. I stepped outside.

Surprise! Standing next to Alice was a beautiful white cria. I checked, it was a girl. Outside I heard Curt honking his horn. He was ready to leave. I ran down the hill and told him the news. He called work to say he would be late. We gave her Bo-Se and dipped the umbilical. All four front teeth were erupted and her palate was complete. Temperature was good, so was pulse and respirations. She weighed 28 pounds.

61

Llama Babies

She seemed strong. We watched as she nursed all four quarters. There was just one problem. Curt listened to her heart sounds two or three times before he told me.

There was a definite whoosh sound in the heart. OSU had a llama with a major heart murmur. We had both listened to that sloshing sound. This was not just like that. It was smaller, quieter, but it was there. We called the vet to consult. Wait a few days, he said, it might close up.

We waited, watched and listened. In the mean time I called OSU and read everything I could find on heart murmurs. I had a list of questions. Most of them went unanswered. We were told it might close on its own, it didn't. We were told she would not be able to run and play. She could keep up with anybody in the herd. She loved to run and dance. We were told she would pant and turn blue, she never did. We were told not to expect her to live. She was strong and healthy. No one could tell us if this murmur was accidental or genetic. There are many ways to get a congenital heart murmur and only some are genetic. No one had done any research on heart murmurs in llamas. Nothing was known about inheritance patterns. Nobody was planning to study heart murmurs like what was being done with the choanal atresia study at OSU. At the time there was no one who wanted her to study heart murmurs. Eventually she was sold as a pet with full disclosure. She is five years old and doing fine.

June 8 1991 Evan: Son of Teenage Mom

Dam's Name:	*Heather*
Baby's Name:	*Evan*
D.O.B.:	*6/8/91*
T.O.B.:	*12 noon*
Sex:	*male*
Weight:	*28 lbs.*
BoSe:	*yes*
Navel:	*Iodine*
Hernia?:	*no*
Teeth:	*all four*
Heart & Lungs:	*good*
Temperature:	*99.2°*
Weather:	*sunny/warm*
Problems / Comments:	*none*

We like to wait until a llama is at least two before we breed her. Many people go by weight. If she is over 200 pounds, go ahead and breed her. Since our adult llamas are large, 200 pounds is not two thirds of their growth. We also prefer spring and summer babies here in the Pacific Northwest. At least then there is a little less rain. But however you try to plan, sometimes the llamas outsmart you.

In March of 91, we acquired an outside breeding to a big name fancy hunk of a stud. We needed to take advantage of this breeding as soon as possible. Heather was our only open llama that fit their requirements. She was 18 months old, a little young by our standards, but just right by the industry standards of the day. We took Heather to the big llama ranch to be bred.

We got a call the next day. Heather was not cooperating. Their vet would check her out. He is a good vet, not the one we regularly use, but one we also like and trust. He called us. Heather was already nine months pregnant. Oops. We felt like child abusers. Needless to say, we brought her home. These things

63

do happen, even in the best of families.

We were worried. Even with ultrasounds we could not tell the due date. Every day we hoped she would go a little bit longer. Would she be able to have this baby without problems? Would she have milk and be able to nurse? Heather was getting lots of practice taking care of her little brother, Chuck. Would she be ready?

We watch her through binoculars from the house. We can see most of the two pastures we use for the girls from the windows of the house. We feel like spies, but it saves trips. She seems to be doing fine. We are more bothered by the event than she is. We have colostrum on hand just in case her milk supply is poor. We know where our vet is at all times. We know where our back up vet is at all times, too. We brace ourselves for what is to come.

We expected the worst. It was fine. We saw the whole thing. No problems. Good sized baby boy. Plenty of milk. Nursed right away. Healthy, active baby. Heather couldn't understand the fuss.

Evan was a very tactile baby. He always slept touching mom or one of his buddies. Other babies may sleep several feet away from their moms. Chuck was always there with him, too. Teenage Heather turned out to be a good mom.

September 7, 1991 Gail: Board Meeting

Dam's Name:	Opal
Baby's Name:	Gail
D.O.B.:	9/7/91
T.O.B.:	1:15 p.m.
Sex:	female
Weight:	25 lbs.
BoSe:	yes
Navel:	Iodine
Hernia?:	no
Teeth:	all four
Heart & Lungs:	good
Temperature:	98.2°
Weather:	sunny/warm
Problems / Comments:	

The Willamette Valley Llama Association board was meeting at our house on Saturday afternoon. We are easy access to I-5 and being in Salem, fairly centrally located. Curt was on the board for about five of its first ten years, first as newsletter editor and later as secretary-treasurer. Both Opal and Mary were expecting any day now. I greeted the guests as I tried to keep an eye on my girls. Once the meeting started, I served refreshments and headed outside.

First, I checked in the barn. A few llamas had taken shelter from the midday sun inside the barn. I went out the double doors. Under some trees we have a sandpile with a sprinkler. Mary was taking advantage of the cool shade, happily chewing her cud, a sure sign she was not in labor. I walked out by the dust bath. Some llamas like to roll in the dust no matter how hot it is. The dust bath is occupied, but not by Opal. She is standing on a small level area by the gate to the backyard, a white cria is hanging three fourths of the way out of her birth canal. As I approached, the baby flopped hard on the ground. I bent to check it out. The little girl was kicking and squirming. She was pink all over.

I ran to the house to get the baby box. I got to the backdoor and it was locked. I pounded hard out of excitement and frustration, forgetting the guests upstairs. I started to move around the house to the front door. Curt stuck his head out a window and saw the baby. Soon the entire WVLA board was standing around Opal and her new baby. The baby was fine. I do not know why I was so bothered by the pink. As soon as she dried off in the sun she fluffed out to look like a normal white llama with gold cheeks.

After Curt had done the honors of the baby routine, the board members went back into the house to finish their meeting. It is amazing how llama people never get tired of seeing new crias arrive, no matter how long they have been in the industry.

We could not figure out a name for this one right away. We called her B-1 for about the first month. At last we settled on Gail.

Curt checking vitals of new cria.

September 8, 1991 George: Foot Injury

Dam's Name:	*Mary*
Baby's Name:	*George*
D.O.B.:	*9/7/91*
T.O.B.:	*12:30 p.m.*
Sex:	*male*
Weight:	*31 lbs.*
BoSe:	*yes*
Navel:	*Iodine*
Hernia?:	*no*
Teeth:	*all four*
Heart & Lungs:	*good*
Temperature:	*100.4°*
Weather:	*overcast, high clouds*
Problems / Comments:	

B-2 was born the very next day. I do not know how people handle having multiple babies on the same day. Two days in a row was enough excitement for me. Besides, I want to enjoy each and every one of them individually. I love to watch the little ones learn to run and play. This was Mary's 5th baby. A brown and white paint destined to be a big packer. He looked very similar to Evan. I was hoping for a matched pair for a double hitch. I was to be disappointed because this little guy turned out to be much bigger than his buddy.

Mary gave birth quickly and easily at 12:30 Sunday afternoon. The day was around 70 and the sky was overcast, a nice day for early September. Everything went smoothly. We could not think of a name for this one either so he went down in the book as B-2, until we could come up with a suitable one. B-2 was a very friendly and active baby. B-2 lead a normal, happy cria life until he had a run-in with the polywire.

Curt and I spearheaded the first three annual WVLA-OSU Llama Herd Health Seminars. In arranging for all the speakers for the full day conference we were introduced to an expert in pasture management. He convinced us to try some more intensive pasture management techniques which he was sure would work as well with llamas as they do with sheep. Using electric polywire portable fencing, our pastures were divided into smaller areas for grazing. When one area was grazed down we moved the llamas on to the next area. It meant we were moving polywire every 2-3 days. At first it looked like a good set up. Llamas ate more grass and needed less hay. However, the whole thing did not account for the nature of llamas.

One section blocked off from the llamas by polywire contained two old apple trees. The llamas were able to ignore this fact until October when the apples were ripe. Three strands of polywire on fiberglass poles makes about a 4 foot fence. The adult llamas began hopping the polywire to get apples.

I got home one Friday afternoon and saw B-2 laying in the pasture caught in the polywire. It was a hot day, over 90°, and he was in full sun. I had no idea how long he had been there. I jumped out of my car and ran to the rescue.

The wire had pulled free of its electrical connection, so he was not electrocuted. I began unwrapping him from the wire. It was wrapped around his body a couple of times. Then I saw his foot and my heart went cold. The wire, with its stainless steel threads, had wrapped tightly around a rear foot like a tourniquet. I knew from first aid that releasing a tourniquet could be a problem. However, in this case there was no wound. I felt the foot. It was not cold. The sun was so hot I could not tell how much circulation had been cut off. Polywire is nearly impossible to break with your bare hands because of the stainless steel. B-2 was squirming too much for me to leave him there while I made a trip to the house for wire cutters. I looked around for something to use as a tool. For some unknown reason, my purse was lying on the grass beside us. I do not know what caused me to bring it with me from the car. I dumped it out on the grass. There was my Swiss army knife. I managed to cut B-2 free and carry him to the barn. He was heavy.

I called the vet and explained what had happened. There were raw scrapes from the binding of the wire, but no open wounds. The foot and leg were swelling quickly. Should I bring him in? No. Just stall rest and watch him carefully. He was to have penicillin, and I needed to monitor his temperature in case of infection. Administer ice or cool soak for the swelling, warm soaks for a few days after that. B-2 would probably benefit most from rest and tincture of time.

Everything went fine until Monday afternoon. Curt was teaching an evening computer class. I soaked B-2's foot in a warm bucket of Epsom's salts. He was so good standing there with his foot in the bucket. I started to dry it off, when I noticed the bottom of his foot. The pads of both toes were starting to slough. Until now there had been no evidence of a wound. Closed wounds can be more dangerous than open ones. I started to panic. This could be the first sign of a nasty infection. If this guy lost his foot, that would be the end of him. I took a deep breath. Curt could not be reached. He would not be home until 10:00 P.M. I had to figure this one out by myself. I knew I had checked the leg before putting the foot in the warm water. There was not any swelling and it was not hot. I took his temperature, normal. I called the vet. He was out on farm calls. He would be back at 6:00 P.M. His car phone was out of range and he could not understand what I was saying. I said I would meet him at his house.

I loaded B-2 into the back of the van and headed down I-5, 40 miles to Corvallis. I pulled in his driveway and waited. The vet pulled in a few minutes later. I tried to explain what was wrong, but he did not get the sense of what I was saying. He went in the house to wash up. When he came out, he said he'd wash the foot with tincture of iodine. It was dusk and the light was not very good, even with the dome light in the van. I got out my flashlight and illuminated the foot. The vet lifted a corner of skin. It was worse than

Llama Babies

I thought. The thick pads of the toes were detached everywhere but around the edges.

We carried B-2 into the barn where there was light. We sedated him and the vet proceeded to cut away the dead tissue. It was a major wound, but there did not appear to be any infection. The dressing on the foot would need to be changed twice a day. The foot needed to be soaked daily in a special bath. Most important, the foot needed to be kept dry during the day.

The rains come to stay for the winter by the first of November. Keeping that foot dry became a real trick. I made a boot out of waterproof cordura for the sole, gortex for the top, and polar fleece lining. I ended up with about six of them because I always needed to put on a clean, dry one and the outsides got really muddy. Twice a day I would dress the wound, bind it with a Teflon no stick pad and gauze, cover that with a clean child's tube sock to absorb the sweat, and put on the boot over all of that. The boot had loop fasteners and I wrapped the top with vet wrap. Most days it would stay on. Some days he lost it in the mud. Then I would have to scrub the foot out with betadine to get it good and clean.

B-2, now George, had to wear the boot for three months. I thought his foot would never heal. It had to be trimmed one or two more times. Eventually it just grew back, as good as new. What a relief.

Did all that handling make this guy berserk? Absolutely not. He became a commercial packer. He was later purchased by one of his clients who fell in love with him. He packs regularly in the Cascades. He is well trained and polite. He gets along with his trail buddies, two retired humans and a gelding llama. He will hand you his feet when you say foot. His owners are looking forward to little Georges to fill out their pack string.

Breeding Goals

Every farm that chooses to breed llamas needs to have a clearly thought out set of breeding goals. It is good for goals to be in written form. Goals can help in making decisions. They help us keep on our chosen path. They give us a sence of accomplishment.

Breeding goals do not need to be complicated. Here are some possible examples:

• We breed single coated, long wooled llamas for hand spinning fleeces.

• We breed tall, short wooled, pack llamas with excellent disposition and confirmation.

• We provide breeding stock with reproductive fitness.

• We specialize in Chilean breeding stock. Notice that some of these goals exclude one another. What is appropriate at one farm may not be desireable at the next. All breeding programs should have some common goals such as these:

• Good health
• Conformation
• Reproductive fitness
•Disposition

At A+ Llamas our breeding program provides a solid foundation of health, reproductive fitness, conformation, disposition, size and bone. We sell pets, trained packers, and breeding stock. Most of our llamas are large, short to medium wooled animals.

CHAPTER 7- 1992

March 7, 1992 Judy: There From Start to Finish

Dam's Name:	*Irene*
Baby's Name:	*Judy*
D.O.B.:	*3/7/92*
T.O.B.:	*10:30 a.m.*
Sex:	*female*
Weight:	*35.5 lbs.*
BoSe:	*yes*
Navel:	*Iodine*
Hernia?:	*no*
Teeth:	*all four*
Heart & Lungs:	*good*
Temperature:	*96.6°*
Weather:	*high overcast, 60°*
Problems / Comments:	*temp o.k. by evening*

Saturday, March 7, Irene went into labor about 10:00 A.M. It was a pleasant spring day, high overcast with temperature near 60°. Irene is very athletic and never slows down for a baby. She delivered this one at 10:30 A.M. The baby weighed 35.5 pounds, a mostly white appaloosa female. Curt dipped the navel while we were waiting for the placenta to pass. He did the BoSe and listened for heart and lung sounds. The Temperature was a bit low so we dried her off with towels and a hair dryer. We no longer give routine enemas. The placenta passed at noon, full and complete. It went into the freezer. So far we have never used one for anything. Every once in a while I have provided placentas to OSU for student use. They are easier to put out Friday mornings with the trash pick up frozen solid.

Baby Judy nursed right after the placenta passed. We even collected a few ounces of colostrum for future use. The best colostrum comes from older moms because they have developed more immunities. I put it in a two ounce container and froze it right away.

A good birth from a good mom is pretty routine stuff. We do not get to see many of them be born. Irene does not mind us being with her. She is a super mom. I am so glad I did not sell her when Curt told me I had to start selling llamas if I was going to be a business. That is what being a llama breeder is all about, isn't it?

Head and toes protrude from mom. Most llama mamas prefer having babies in the open pasture. It usually is a much cleaner environment than in a barn.

March 16, 1992 Erin 6:30 A.M. Repeats Itself.

Dam's Name:	*Alice*
Baby's Name:	*Erin*
D.O.B.:	*3/16/92*
T.O.B.:	*early morning*
Sex:	*female*
Weight:	*30 lbs.*
BoSe:	*yes*
Navel:	*Iodine*
Hernia?:	*no*
Teeth:	*slightly erupted*
Heart & Lungs:	*good*
Temperature:	*98.8°*
Weather:	*42° overcast*
Problems / Comments:	*rt. ear folded against head*

Alice appears to have fallen into a pattern of early morning babies. It's Monday morning and time for Curt to leave for work. We are on baby watch for Alice. I rush out to the barn to check on her before Curt leaves. Here I am in nightgown, boots and bathrobe, hoping nobody sees me waving my flashlight around. Alice has come in already. She is standing at the manger eating hay. Tucked under her, nursing, is a female cria. I can see it is a girl right away because her tail is curled up over her back. I grab a plastic garbage bag and a rubber glove from the baby box and head up the hill to look for the placenta. I find it right away under one of the big fir trees. I put the glove on and lift it into the bag, examining it for wholeness as I go. It is already cold. The baby probably was born between 2 and 3 A.M. It is 42°, fairly mild for a spring morning. No frost. The sky is beginning to look slightly overcast.

I get Curt. He hurries and does the honors, BoSe, iodine, checks for hernia, heart and lung sounds. The teeth are only slightly erupted. One ear is still tightly folded against the head. She weighs 30 pounds. Curt is efficient. He's off to work in time to teach his first class. I grab the Polaroid and snap a picture of Erin to take to work.

Pregnancy Testing

There are many ways to confirm pregnancy in llamas.

1. *Check with the male.* Llamas usually know if a female is pregnant or open. Most female llamas will spit off a male and refuse to sit down 3 to 4 weeks into pregnancy. This method is a problem with very aggressive males or if the females like the male too much. Either way the male may breed a pregnant female. We have had both problems. Also some females spit off males as a matter of personality.

2. *Blood tests.* Either the vet draws the blood and sends it to a lab or you can do it yourself. We draw blood from the ear and send it to Napa Valley Laboratories in special little vials. We get about a four day turn around. They measure for progesterone levels. Progesterone is a steroid and does not degrade over the few days it takes to get the sample processed. This test can be done as early as 21 days after last breeding. Some sources recommend 30 to 45 days.

3. *Rectal Palpation.* The vet does this examination by reaching into the rectum and feeling the reproductive tract. It works best 45 to 60 days after breeding. You get your results instantly. Rectal palpation can cause a rectal tear.

4. *Ultrasound.* The vet places a probe into the rectum and the uterus is displayed on a screen. It requires skill and practice and the equipment is very expensive. The results are immediate.

5. *Trans-abdominal ultrasound.* I like this idea the best, but it needs more work. The probe is placed on the abdomen and is non invasive. The equipment is very expensive and requires much skill and experience. The images are harder to interpret. It does not work in llamas the same way as in people because the distances are greater.

6. *Binocular method.* Toes protruding out from under female's tail.

Legs and head are out. Dam is standing.

June 16, 1992 Alma's Baby Boy Surprise

Dam's Name:	*Alma*
Baby's Name:	*Surprise*
D.O.B.:	*6/16/92*
T.O.B.:	*daytime*
Sex:	*male*
Weight:	*33 lbs.*
BoSe:	*yes*
Navel:	*Iodine*
Hernia?:	*no*
Teeth:	*all four*
Heart & Lungs:	*good*
Temperature:	*101°*
Weather:	*70° high overcast*
Problems / Comments:	

We tried breeding Alma for a spring baby, but it just would not take. We did preg checks in October, and the vet said she was not pregnant. We rebred her in October. She went down for the male three times before she spit him off. The vet checked her in December and confirmed the October pregnancy. We decided to sell two girls at the Firecracker. Anyone due in June, July or August was out of the question. Alma was picked because of her October due date.

The Firecracker requires a verification of pregnancy within 30 days of the show. The vet came, checked her over and signed a paper with the October due date.

As soon as school was out for the summer I was working with my sale girls everyday to make sure they could load, walk on lead, be touched, and be presented in the sale ring. Alma was athletic like her mom, but she was having problems with a jump I was asking her to do. She started to complain and lie down. I was worried. Something was wrong. I told Curt I was afraid she was going to miscarry because she was showing pink where she should have been tight. I decided to back off on the jumps.

That afternoon about 4:30P.M. we found a strange cria near the barn. Surprise was up and dry, walking around. It did not take us long to figure out that this dark brown 33 pound boy belonged to Alma. So much for rectals, ultra sounds, and checking with a male. This was no October baby.

I called Dick Wickum to tell him what had happened. I offered to withdraw her from the sale and substitute a different female. He said no, bring her anyway. I don't approve of last trimester llamas being brought to sales. It is just too stressful. I've seen some abort. Now I was embarrassed to have to present my mistake to the entire llama community. Dick said not to worry. Catalog due dates are frequently way off. Some people are really attracted to those babies. I was thankful the baby came two weeks before the sale and not at it.

This dam is in a sitting position. Dams will get up and down and sometimes even roll with cria partially out.

July 7, 1992 First Loss

Heather picked the place she wanted to have her baby. It was in the newer half of the barn, the lighter side, more airy. She had pulled hay down onto the floor of the barn and made herself a nest. About ten o'clock in the morning she started to hum. She was elongated and showing pink. She sat in the barn facing the manger. She didn't roll or do much up down movement. She was not eating or chewing her cud. I could tell by her hum she was unhappy. She was not making any progress. I sat with her the whole time. I don't get much opportunity to be with my girls when they deliver. About eleven I called the vet. He was with another client and would come when he could. I still was not too worried. I had taken LaRue Johnson's Neonatal Clinic and one from OSU as well. I had my baby box full of goodies. I felt prepared.

About eleven, she seemed to loose all interest. I could not see any more contractions. She rested, cushed in her nest. I called the vet. Scrub up and go in, was the word. I'd already clipped and filed my nails. I scrubbed up, put on gloves and OB sleeve. By now Heather was standing. I reached in. Two feet and a nose. I pulled my hand out. Whoosh! The placenta was lying at my feet. Panic rose in my throat. I reached in again and grabbed those feet. The baby seemed to be in the right position. I checked, yes, I had front legs, not rear. I pulled. Nothing. I rotated a little in case there was hip lock and pulled some more. I checked again, nose was there, neck was not twisted, however there was no movement from the baby. I tugged and tugged. Finally the head slipped out. I cleared the mouth. Nothing. I checked its eyes. Odd, one was blue and one was white. We did not have any blue eyes in our herd. The eyes stared back at me dead. I was too late.

There was nothing I could do for the baby. Now I had to worry about Heather. Should I continue to pull or let her be? I let her rest for a while. Finally, she got back up and started to push. I pulled. We worked and worked. At last, the baby lay still on the floor. Heather laid down. I sat in the manger, too tired to cry.

Curt and the vet arrived at the same time that afternoon. They weighed the baby. It was big, 40 pounds. Too big. The vet had me pack the baby in a box. I asked if it should go to OSU to be necropsied. No, it was unlikely anything more could be discovered. This baby was too big. Its birth was compromised when the placenta passed first. It would be put to better use at the Neonatal Clinic the next day. He made a comment about the odd eyes and then turned to fix up mom.

Heather needed some stitches for some tearing, an accidental episiotomy. Luckily there was no internal tears. Heather was bruised and swollen. If I ever have to pull another cria I will use even more J-lube than I did this time. The vet gave her something for pain, something to help dry her up, and two weeks of antibiotics to prevent infection. She'd need a vaginal examine before rebreeding.

For months afterwards Heather would whinny and rush to check out every new youngster that came on the place. She looked for that baby until she had her next one. I know the vet said it was best to get the dead baby away immediately, but I wonder. I do not think she accepted that it was dead. Heather has never let me around her babies again.

August 30, 1992 Harold: Future Cart Llama

Dam's Name:	*Opal*
Baby's Name:	*Harold*
D.O.B.:	*8/30/92*
T.O.B.:	*11:30 a.m.*
Sex:	*male*
Weight:	*30 lbs.*
BoSe:	*yes*
Navel:	*Iodine*
Hernia?:	*no*
Teeth:	*yes*
Heart & Lungs:	*good*
Temperature:	*97.7°*
Weather:	*70° overcast*
Problems / Comments:	

Opal has been very cooperative in having her babies when we are around to watch. It was a moderate summer day , high overcast with some clouds, 70°, nice Willamette Valley weather. Opal went into labor a little after 10:30 A.M. It lasted less than an hour. Out came a 30 pound baby boy, appy like mom and dad, a future packer/cart llama like his dad, grandsire, and great grand sire before that.

We decided right away to hold this male back. We wanted to teach him to pack and to cart. How many fourth generation cart llamas are out there?

A cart llama first needs to be a wonderful Public Relations llama. Harold's training started early. He learned to ride in the van and in the back of the pickup truck when he was still small enough to be lifted in. We took him to fairs, fund raising events, and parades when he was old enough to leave mom. The summer he was a year old, we tied him to the back of the pack string when we went hiking. He learned to do obstacle courses both with and without packs. He learned to work with all kinds of people from kids to adults.

Harold shines as a pack llama. At four he has three seasons on the trail behind him. He loves to go packing. He never complains about his load or the steepness of the trail. He still has a few skills to polish up on. His youthful strength and exuberance sometimes get the best of him. He loves to camp out and does not need to be staked or picketed at night.

Harold is just about ready to start ground driving. Because of his high spirits, we delayed a bit in moving to this step. We want driving to be a positive experience for both llama and people.

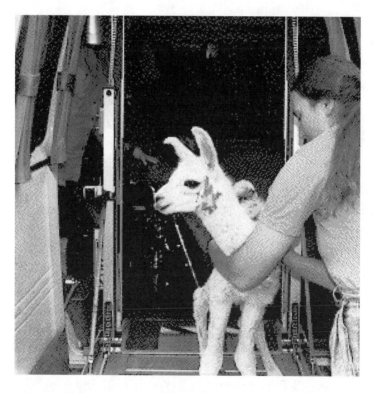

Harold (at two days of age) visiting a handicapped access van.

83

September 12, 1992 Zack: Umbilical Breaks

Dam's Name:	Mary
Baby's Name:	Zack
D.O.B.:	9/12/92
T.O.B.:	1:40 p.m.
Sex:	male
Weight:	30 lbs.
BoSe:	yes
Navel:	Iodine
Hernia?:	no
Teeth:	yes
Heart & Lungs:	good
Temperature:	97.9°
Weather:	60° showers
Problems / Comments:	umbilical broke open

Mary considerately had her sixth baby on a weekend so we could be around. She had this one in the barn. There had been showers earlier in the day. High temperature was 60 with cloudy skies. Weather in the Willamette valley is fairly moderate year round. September is not a bad time for babies in this part of the country. Everything went smoothly. The boy cria was on the ground by 1:40 P.M. Curt decided our barn scale was not working so he picked the little guy up and carried him into the house to use our doctor's scale. With his arms full of squirming cria, Curt left the door and the gate open. I followed him when I noticed. I did not want the llamas to get out. I got to the barn door and looked down. I saw blood, bright red, fresh blood. I ran to the gate. More blood. It was dripping heavily. I called out to Curt and ran to catch up. I followed the trail of blood up the stairs to the kitchen. The baby was fighting being carried, throwing himself around. I called Curt's attention to the blood. His face blanched. He had not seen it. What had happened?

Curt's belt buckle had caught the umbilical cord

as the baby fought being carried. The umbilical broke open. Llama blood is so much thicker and brighter than human blood, that I am not certain that the baby bled as profusely as I thought it did. Curt put direct pressure on the umbilical to stop the bleeding. I grabbed the dental floss and more iodine. When the bleeding stopped, I helped Curt tie off the umbilical twice. Curt held a gauze pad on the wound for some time while I mopped up the blood. We redipped the umbilical and carried the baby back out to mom.

This is an example of a problem caused by too much human interference. If Curt could have let things go and not hurried to weigh the baby right now, this would not have happened. The umbilical would have sealed off and been much less vulnerable had we waited.

Torsion

Torsion is when the uterus gets twisted. The twist can be right or left with a range of 90° to 360° rotation. The greater the twist, the more serious the situation. Experiencing a torsion can be very

CHAPTER 8- 1993

March 1, 1993 Wally: Torsion

Dam's Name:	*Tana*
Baby's Name:	*Wally*
D.O.B.:	*3/1/93*
T.O.B.:	*8:10 p.m.*
Sex:	*male*
Weight:	*26.5 lbs.*
BoSe:	*yes*
Navel:	*Iodine*
Hernia?:	*major, 2 inch*
Teeth:	*yes*
Heart & Lungs:	*good*
Temperature:	*98.9°*
Weather:	*mild*
Problems / Comments:	*assisted*

We had our first spring baby of 93 on March 1. We have four more due within a week, if I figured things out right. We thought grouping our births would be a good idea, but I have since changed my mind. We do not have the resources to deal with more than one crisis at a time. We will be in big trouble if we have any problems. The first 93 birth proved that. We ended up with a torsion of sorts.

Tana had two possible due dates, February 15 and March 11. We had a male injure himself on a fence, so we had to switch males in the middle of our breeding season. The injured male had bloody semen. Blood kills sperm. The vet did not think the first breedings could have taken. He thought he would be able to tell the due dates from the ultra sounds. He advised us to just switch and keep breeding without a break between males. Guess what! He couldn't tell from the ultra sounds. We started baby watch on

February 6. We were concerned because Tana had not had a baby in some time.

The 15th passed, so we figured to start watching again around March 2. She didn't look ready to have her baby, however, shortly after that she had a slight accident. It was sunny and warm. Tana had found a small dry patch in the snow covered pasture. She was laying in the afternoon sunshine on the hillside. She decided to roll. She slipped on the ice and got stuck on her back. Curt saw it happen, but he came in the house to get me to roll her up. He and Tana do not see eye to eye. She gets mad at him. I ran out. She was stuck. After a couple of false starts, I flipped her up. I called the vet and waited to see what would happen. She appeared to be fine. I thought I had over reacted.

On February 27, Tana had another problem. In the evenings, she gets fed in a stall with two other pushy eaters. I fed them first. Then I fed the rest of the girls and went out and fed the boys. To let the girls out of the barn when I came back, I opened all of the gates. Most of them were still eating hay. Tana chased everybody out of her stall. She sat down humming and panting like she was going into labor. This was about 6 P.M., so I called the vet. He had Curt check her vitals and decided it was a false alarm. She had the same behavior the next day, so I decided I would have to feed her separately until her baby came. On the first, Curt came home early because he had some minor surgery. About 3:30 P.M. he decided Tana was going into labor. He was concerned because it was late in the day and it didn't match up to either possible breeding date. I got home an hour later. I called the vet and told him to be ready for a dystocia, a difficult birth. He felt it was too early to call it that. He said he would check back at 6 P.M. and could be there at 8 P.M. I told him to plan on it.

I called the Wilsons and said we were having a problem birth that evening. I left a message that they could come watch and help. We would be in the barn, doing what needed to be done. Tana has a long, narrow pelvis and weighs 400 lbs. Rolling her, while holding the baby, was not going to be easy, even with four helpers.

The Vet arrived around 8 P.M., the Wilson's right behind him. We put Tana in the chute. He gave her a drug to keep her feet planted while he did an examination. He could feel the constricted uterus through the rectal wall, but he was having a hard time figuring out how much twist there was. He decided to do a vaginal to see if she was dilated. The cervix was open. That meant the baby didn't have much chance. What was confusing him was that the twist went the wrong direction, not the usual way. Because of that, it was only about 180° instead of 360°. He was able to reach in and turn the baby and the uterus, reducing the torsion. The baby popped out. It shot across the barn about ten feet hitting Curt in the chest. It was white and male. We were all surprised when it started to wiggle.

I stayed up until two making sure it nursed and mom was all right. We just can't have two like that in the same day. I look at the calendar. We have four due at any time. They could all come on one day. What would I do then?

I guess this is more proof to Murphy's Llama Law: White male babies never die.

Wally had one additional problem. He was born with about a two inch umbilical hernia, too big to close without some help. The danger with a hernia this size is that guts can get caught in it, get pinched off, resulting in serious infection and even death. A friend had successfully treated a similar case by using a specially constructed harness to keep constant pressure on the opening. A tennis ball was sewed into the harness to apply the pressure. I borrowed the harness and gave it a try. Wally was like Houdini and the straight jacket. No matter how we pinned and taped that harness on, he was out of it as soon as we were out of sight. We tried and tried to no avail.

Eventually the hernia was corrected surgically when he was five and a half months old. There was no material protruding through the opening, so it was an easy procedure.

Umbilical Hernias

Llama babies, like human babies, can be born with umbilical hernias where the opening around the navel fails to close at birth. These things usually close off in a few months. If it fails to close, it can be corrected surgically. All babies should be checked for hernias. Discuss your options with your veterinarian.

Isn't life great?

March 6, 1993 Bob: Blood!

Dam's Name:	*Betty*
Baby's Name:	*Bob*
D.O.B.:	*3/6/93*
T.O.B.:	*12:30 p.m.*
Sex:	*male*
Weight:	*26 lbs.*
BoSe:	*yes*
Navel:	*Iodine*
Hernia?:	*no*
Teeth:	*all four*
Heart & Lungs:	*good*
Temperature:	*99.8°*
Weather:	*50° overcast*
Problems / Comments:	*assisted with mild rotation*

The WVLA has its annual Stud Auction and Banquet each spring to raise money for llama research. We have raised more money for research than any other local association. We would like to challenge other associations to do the same. This is the big event of our social calendar. For several years the affair has been held at a hotel in Wilsonville. They let us bring the studs right into the dining hall. We are on baby watch, but plan to attend.

Betty is a first time mom. She was bred at 18 months, the popular industry standard of the day. She is at 342 days gestation, well within the window of 350 plus or minus ten days. She decides to have her baby on Stud Auction Day. I am out cleaning the barn when Betty goes into labor. Up and down. Two feet and a nose. The baby is turned slightly in the birth canal, feet presented slightly above the head. When it became apparent it was not going to come any further without assistance, I rotated it and it popped right out. It seemed to be in a shoulder lock. The vet was unavailable. I waited until baby's breathing appeared to be compromised, it was becoming irregular, so I acted. I did not use any force. Some blood passed with the placenta. I noticed that the baby did not have his caps on his toes. Llamas are born with rubbery little slippers on there feet that protect the inside of the uterus and birth canal. The baby was a cute woolly white male. Betty appeared to be fine. She was fine at 5 P.M. Baby was very active and nursing. We left for the Stud Auction.

We drove up the driveway at 11:00P.M. The baby was running around in the field. We could see him in our headlights. Something was wrong. I rolled down my window and pulled out a flashlight. Betty was cushed, but things did not look right. Curt took the flashlight and walked up the hill. He found Betty lying in a pool of blood.

I went back and got the van. I drove it up through the field next to where Betty was lying. Thank goodness for four wheel drive. Curt and I struggled to load the unconscious llama into the back of the van. It took a long time. We put the baby in, too. We went back to the house and called OSU. We told the vet student on night duty we were coming in. All the llama specialists were still at the party. We had left early. We would have to settle for the doctor on call until morning. As tired as we were, we drove the 45 miles to the vet school. The fog was so thick we could barely see.

The doctor on call was a horse vet from Kentucky. He had some llama experience, but this was his first time on call since he started his new job. Some students helped us load Betty onto a cart and we rolled her in through the big door. Curt went with a student to find a safe place for the baby. The horse vet lead the way into the horse side of the hospital. He indicated a huge horse chute. I told him no. It was okay to use a chute, but we would use the llama chute in the freshly remodeled llama wing in the other end of the hospital. The new guy did not know what I was talking about.

"Come with me," I said. "The WVLA just finished paying for this thing tonight, and you're going to be one of the first to use it."

I rolled my llama through the halls to the other side of the hospital. A research llama occupied one of the stalls, but everything else was brand new, waiting to be used. A new chute stood in the middle of the examination area. I went in a small storage area and pulled out a cart loaded with all the llama sized tools the vet would need for his examination. Dr. Kentucky looked slightly bemused. "I had an early tour," I said, "You're new. You'll have to get used to llama people."

The horse vet proceeded to do a vaginal examination. Blood had pooled in the back of the vagina and in the uterus, but he could not tell where it had come from. There was too much swelling. He packed the vagina. Betty would have to have an IV for fluids, antibiotics, and painkiller. After the swelling went down she could be examined by a reproduction specialist. If the blood came from a vaginal tear, she would heal and be fine. If it was a tear in the uterus, the prognosis was much worse.

It was about 3:00 A.M. when we were ready to leave. We walked out the door into fog so thick we could not see across the parking lot. There was no way either of us could drive home safely as tired as we were. I had wrapped Betty in a sleeping bag and some blankets for the ride to the vet school. We climbed in the back of the van and went to sleep. We woke up in the morning when the fog started to lift. We went in and checked on Betty and Bob one more time. This time she was alert and recognized us. She had an IV line dripping into her neck and Bob was nursing.

As it turned out Betty and her baby Bob stayed at the hospital four days at a cost of $700. Bob was fine, and so were his IgG levels. Mom had a small tear in her vaginal wall which nearly caused her to bleed to death. A month later, when everything had healed, Betty was again examined by the reproductive specialist and pronounced ready to rebred.

March 7, 1993 Karen: Fast

Dam's Name:	*Alice*
Baby's Name:	*Karen*
D.O.B.:	*3/7/93*
T.O.B.:	*noon*
Sex:	*female*
Weight:	*31 lbs.*
BoSe:	*yes*
Navel:	*Iodine*
Hernia?:	*no*
Teeth:	*all four*
Heart & Lungs:	*good*
Temperature:	*99.3°*
Weather:	*50°*
Problems / Comments:	*short labor*

Sunday we are still recovering from our all night vigil. Betty and Bob are still at the vet school. Curt and I are trying to get some rest. Tomorrow is work as usual.

Alice finally decided to have her baby at a normal time. It was noon on Sunday, we were home, and we did not see a thing. I had my eye on Alice. She was at 345 days and looked about to deliver. She was sitting in the upper pasture leaning against the big maple tree. I saw Alice get up and walk into the barn. Nothing was showing. Curt walked into the barn maybe 5 minutes later and the baby was on the ground. Alice was standing. By 12:20 the baby was standing. Curt did the routine, temperature, heart and lung sounds, teeth, no hernia, BoSe and iodine. By 2:00 the baby had nursed, but we had not seen the placenta. The placenta finally passed between 2:00 and 2:30.

This was our first baby out of a new Chilibol, Chilean Bolivian cross, stud. She looked just like mom. We were not impressed with what he added, but we planned to give him a few more tries.

Here is a letter I wrote at the time:

When it rains it pours. I know where that came from now. I have a new one.**Don't plan to have all your babies at the same time.** Spread your resources. Somebody told me it was such a good idea. It sounded good at the time. We had 23 babies before we ever lost one last July. Then babies number 26 and 27 both have problems. Lucky for us we were here for all three. We like March babies because we are home 50 per cent of the time in March. Having to stay up all night two nights in one week is a problem. We are very lucky both babies are strong and healthy. Baby 28 came out fine.

I hope you are up to reading chaotic organization. I'm not doing too hot on linear thinking tonight. Curt has had to go to California to take care of his folks. They are both sick. He'll be gone almost two weeks. I'm staying home for spring break waiting for the next two babies. I've screwed up on their due dates so I don't know when they will be here. I tried calling the vet, but he is on vacation for a week. They both had positive ultrasounds last May or so, so they should be here by April 1, maybe. As long as nothing goes wrong, I should be OK. I think I'll keep the new moms in the barn the first few nights. If I sleep in the barn, I shouldn't have any post birth surprises. I could never load an unconscious llama into the van by myself.

Sincerely,
Barbara Anderson

April 2 1993 Irving: Heat Lamp

Dam's Name:	Irene
Baby's Name:	Irving
D.O.B.:	4/2/93
T.O.B.:	daytime
Sex:	male
Weight:	37 lbs.
BoSe:	yes
Navel:	Iodine
Hernia?:	no
Teeth:	all four
Heart & Lungs:	good/cough
Temperature:	99.1°
Weather:	55° rainy
Problems / Comments:	cough gone by 6 p.m.

April 2 was 55° and rainy, not the kind of day Curt would predict for a llama baby. Irene was at 346 days and I was on baby watch. I found Irving when I got home from work at 4:00 P.M. He was up and the placenta had already passed. I brought him into the house to dry him off with towels and the hair dryer. His temperature was 99.1° and he had a little cough. Irving was a very loud appaloosa, the third appy baby produced by this pair of brown llamas. He weighed 37 pounds. All four teeth were erupted. Except for the cough, he looked in good shape. I took him back out to the barn after doing BoSe and Iodine. I put him and mom into a stall and replaced the light in the fixture with a heat lamp. I brought out a book and a chair and waited for him to nurse. At 6:18 P.M. he nursed all four quarters. The cough was gone. I turned off the heat lamp and waited for the bulb to cool before putting back in the regular one and taking the heat lamp back to the house.

I have heard much discussion about heat lamps in barns. They are not the best choice. If one breaks, the bulb explodes sending hot glass everywhere. They can start barn fires. Adult llamas can knock them down. If you mount them in a safe permanent fixture, they usually are to far away to do any good.

Thermoregulation in Neonates

Veterinary medicine is full of big word that ordinary people must translate to useful language. What this means is new crias can not control their own body heat. Do not let new crias lie in the hot sun. Keep them out of chilling winds, rain and snow. Do not cook them with heating pads.

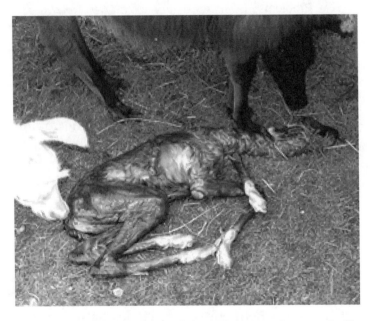

This cria just hit the ground. She is still wet and covered with membrane and has soft caps on her feet.

April 9, 1993 Linda: Cria Comes to Dinner

Dam's Name:	*Nancy*
Baby's Name:	*Linda*
D.O.B.:	*4/9/93*
T.O.B.:	*7:40 p.m.*
Sex:	*female*
Weight:	*29.5 lbs.*
BoSe:	*yes*
Navel:	*Iodine*
Hernia?:	*no*
Teeth:	*yes*
Heart & Lungs:	*good*
Temperature:	*99.6°*
Weather:	*44° rainy*
Problems / Comments:	*dried baby, milked out wax plugs, stalled for night*

A week later Linda came to a first time mom. We had purchased Nancy at as a yearling to breed to Chaucer, our big Fortunato son. Chaucer, however , put himself out of the stud business by not quite making it jumping over a fence. We then went out and acquired a couple of young stud prospects, a Bolivian and a Chilibol. Linda was the second baby to hit the ground out of the Chilibol.

New moms do not know all the rules of when llamas have babies. April 9 was 44 degrees and raining. I called the girls into the barn to eat at 7:30 P.M. I divide up the barn into sections at mealtime so I can contain the pushiest eaters and make sure everyone gets her correct ration. Nancy went to her assigned place to gobble her meal. She had barely got it down when, oops, here comes baby, right in the middle of the crowd. I ushered the rest of the girls to the other side of the barn. The new cria was a bright red girl with nice fiber. I went to the house to get the baby box, towels and hair dryer.

I dried baby off and dipped the navel in iodine. Next came BoSe and temperature. I put mom and baby, Linda, in a stall for the night. I did not want baby out in the rain. I put the heat bulb into the fixture.

I checked Nancy's udder. It was hard to the touch. I went in the house and got a warm, wet hand towel. I packed it into a thermos full of warm water. Back in the stall, I carefully held the warm cloth on the udder for a few minutes. I reached under and milked the wax plugs out of her teats. I rinsed out the cloth and cleaned off Nancy's rear. The placenta still had to pass.

I went back to the house for my sleeping bag, pillow, and book. I settled down in the manger to wait and watch for the baby to nurse. It did not take long for the placenta to pass. I checked it and packed it into a large plastic bag. It would get labeled and go into the freezer. Baby was checking out the dark corners of the stall. I guided her over to mom and gently shoved her under. On about the third try she connected. Both Curt and I have great success with this method of encouragement. It works fine as long as the human or mom do not get too anxious. In the human environment of a stall there are so many shadows and man-made things that baby can get confused and waste valuable time cribbing in all the wrong places. This will not happen if you leave mom and baby out in the field on a clear day. This was a rainy night and we had to make do. I felt a little assistance was in order and it worked.

I settled down for a night in the barn. I wanted to be sure baby got it right the next time on her own.

Colostrum

Colostrum is the first milk produced after birthing. It is rich in immunoglobulin which primes the cria's immune system. It is essential that llama babies get adequate intake of colostrum during the first 24 hours of life. The best absorption of the big Ig molecules happens during the first six hours and decreases from there.

Babies that fail to nurse adequately in the first 6-8 hours need to be supplemented. Discuss your options with your vet ahead of time and be prepared. Goat or cow colostrum can be used as a substitute provided it is from a well vaccinated herd and is actual first milking. Powdered substitutes are inadequate.

Colostrum may be frozen and keeps for years. Freeze it in small amounts, 1-2 oz. or even ice cube trays. Seal the containers well and be sure to date and label each one. Thaw out what you need by placing it on the kitchen counter or putting the bottle in warm water. Do not put colostrum in the microwave as it kills it.

A 30 pound baby will need 3 pints of colostrum, given in a total of 6 feedings over the first 12 hours. Always use mom's colostrum first if it is available and for some reason the baby can not nurse. It is best for the baby to suck it down, but it is possible to tube it. Tubing requires special training.

Babies that do not get enough colostrum can be given a plasma transfer to boost their immune system. This is a medical procedure done by a veterinarian. It is not without risks and costs.

May 24, 1993 Jim: Malmature

Dam's Name:	*Ethyl*
Baby's Name:	*Jim*
D.O.B.:	*5/24/93*
T.O.B.:	*daytime*
Sex:	*male*
Weight:	*22.5 lbs.*
BoSe:	*yes*
Navel:	*Iodine*
Hernia?:	*no*
Teeth:	*no*
Heart & Lungs:	*good*
Temperature:	*100.1°*
Weather:	*80° overcast T-showers*
Problems / Comments:	*malmature, weak*

We had another white male. We found Jim around
4:30 P.M. on my birthday. This was his mom's first
baby and our first out of a new stud. The baby is half
Bolivian. He was premature even though by my
calculations he was full term. Mom couldn't take more
than two weeks of afternoon thunder storms.
However, the baby shifted exactly two weeks before,
which made him right on time. Needless to say, Jim
couldn't nurse because he was not yet ready. His
swallow reflex was very weak and he was too loose
and uncoordinated to stand. His legs would not hold
him up. He was like a rag doll. I had 6 ounces of real
llama colostrum on hand which we coaxed down him
with a bottle. He did not want to swallow and needed
considerable encouragement. It took awhile for
mom's milk to come in. We gave him our supply of
cow colostrum and then switched to a blend of low-
fat milk and yogurt and twice a day mom's llama
milk. He passed his IgG test. Mom's young age
probably contributed. Looking back, I think we
should have waited to breed her. She was only 16
months old when bred. At the time, it was common

to bred as young as 13 months. I guess I got what was coming to me.

The vet called this baby malmature, full term but not ready to come out yet. His cartilage was not solid enough for him to stand. His ears were flopped down on his head. We fed him for five days every four hours except we skipped one feeding while we were at work. It actually worked out to be 3 P.M., 6 P.M.,10 P.M., 2 A.M. and 6 A.M. His suck reflex was so poor that it took a long time to get the amount into him that the vet said he needed to have. In order to fit in the feedings and our work day, we had to adjust our sleep schedule. I did the 6 P.M. feeding, ate dinner and went to bed. I got up at four to milk mom and do the six o'clock feeding. Curt did the afternoon feeding and the one in the middle of the night.

We had to learn how to milk a llama. I called a llama friend to show me how. Instead of trying to sit beside the llama and reach under like a cow, she showed me how to lean over the llama, putting weight of my chest over her hips. The milking hand goes over the back and under on the far side while the other hand reaches under on the near side with a wide mouthed plastic cup to catch the milk. This keeps you close in to the llama and out of the way of being kicked. Llamas don't have much to grab onto. Their utter is more like a cat than a cow. By a combination of massage, pushing and gentle squeezing it was fairly easy to milk a llama in this position. We have not had to do this very often, so we are not experts in this matter. There may be an easier way, but this works and did not seem unpleasant for mom or the milker.

Bottle feeding was a mess. Jim got it all over everything. We would sit on our heels astride the cria, tilting his head up into nursing position, being careful not to put any weight on him. At first he did not have the strength or coordination to fight it. The vet recommended the bottle over tubing because it was important to develop his swallowing and sucking abilities. When we finished, he had to be cleaned up with a warm wash cloth. I would pack one in a thermos to keep it warm. We knew we could not keep this pace up for long.

We had a discussion with the vet. By day five the baby's cartilage had firmed up enough so that he could stand. He liked his mama's milk a whole lot more than the yogurt concoction the vet prescribed. After much debate we decided to withdraw the feedings. Mom had plenty of milk. Either he nursed or he didn't. We fed him one last time, closed the stall door, and left. I was sure he would not choose to nurse. We left them alone for 24 hours. That was very hard for me to do. No peeking, no rescuing. I was sure the baby would be dead when we opened the barn. Surprise! He was standing under mom nursing. What a relief.

We still had more problems ahead. We now let mom and baby out with the other llamas. The vet had said it was good for the baby to be outside on dry days. We don't have many of those in June. As soon as he got outside in the sunshine, he started loosing his hair, a little at first, then all of it. He got badly sunburned. He had to be confined to the barn again. We made him a pen in the shade so he could get outside some. Our vet had never seen this happen. He called around. No one knew what to do. I treated his sunburn with Desidin. OSU was using it for urine burn. It contains zinc oxide to block the sun and it is made for baby skin. After about a month his hair grew back in.

My theory is that Jim had some sort of high fever spike before he was born. It did not happen afterwards because we took his temperature every time we fed him and it was always low normal. Fevers can cause breaks in the wool. His break was under the skin. It took a week or so to get to the surface. The sun did not have anything to do with the hair loss. Exposure to the sun, however, made the problem more serious because of the sunburn.

Another explanation could be that it was all an allergic reaction to the yogurt mix. The sun aggravated the allergy and he became photosensitive. The vet had used this mixture on many babies and he had never had any problems. He has switched since to 5% cows milk.

Today Jim lives with a herd of cows down the road. He had a llama companion, but he prefers to stay with the cows.

A llama sniffs a newly born spotted cria..

August 1, 1993 Patty: Mom in Charge

Dam's Name:	*Gretchen*
Baby's Name:	*Patty*
D.O.B.:	*8/1/93*
T.O.B.:	*11:55 a.m.*
Sex:	*female*
Weight:	*28 lbs.*
BoSe:	*yes*
Navel:	*Iodine*
Hernia?:	*no*
Teeth:	*four*
Heart & Lungs:	*good*
Temperature:	*101.1°*
Weather:	*72° clear-dry*
Problems / Comments:	*none*

Gretchen's last baby was Dec. 2, 1990. She developed milk fever during sub zero weather. We took her to OSU when the baby was 6 weeks old. She had lost about 100 lbs. and had abscesses from the calcium shots. The vet school put her on IV's for a couple of days. They decided there was nothing they could do. She wouldn't eat. Curt had to go down and feed her by hand. They sent her home to die. It took over a year to get her weight up to 300 lbs. so she could be rebred.

This birth was very quick. We were right there the whole time. It lasted about 30 minutes from start to finish. The baby hit the ground at 10:55 A.M. The placenta passed and the baby had nursed by 11:50 A.M.

It is interesting to watch an experienced mom as opposed to a new mother handle her new baby. Gretchen stood directly over her baby at all times until the baby successfully nursed. When Curt sat over the baby to give it her shot, Gretchen climbed over him, too. Each time the baby tried to stand, she propped it up with her leg. She never let it crib on the wall or wander around.

We weighed Gretchen and the baby every day to make sure Gretchen was holding her own and the baby was gaining. We fed Gretchen extra pellets twice a day. We also made a creep feeder available for the baby as soon as she was interested in eating

We did not bred Gretchen back while she was nursing Patty. We waited an entire year, but it still did not take. The vet says Gretchen is fit, but I do not know if she will ever have another cria. I am unwilling to use hormones or drugs on her considering all she has been through. Gretchen is our friend, and not just a baby making machine. She adds common sense and playfulness to our herd and in that way contributes to the well-being of us all.

Patty was sold when she was about two weeks old. She was to be delivered at six months. We had never pre-sold a llama before, but the people had begged. We let them name her. Six months came and they kept putting us off. Eventually they backed out. Part of me was upset because we had passed up several good opportunities to sell her. Curt was delighted. Patty is his special girl and he hopes to keep her forever.

August 5, 1993 Reba

Dam's Name:	*Heather*
Baby's Name:	*Reba*
D.O.B.:	*8/5/93*
T.O.B.:	*discovered 8:30 p.m.*
Sex:	*female*
Weight:	*34 lbs.*
BoSe:	*yes*
Navel:	*Iodine*
Hernia?:	*no*
Teeth:	*all four*
Heart & Lungs:	*good*
Temperature:	*98.2°*
Weather:	*hot day 90+*
Problems / Comments:	

I had to pull Heather's last baby. It was born dead. The placenta detached. I took the dead baby away. I think Heather thinks I stole it. She checked every baby that came along to see if it was hers. This year I was very nervous. We stayed home from LANA to wait for these two babies. I kept checking her every hour. She was sick of me and refused to have it when I was around. She waited until I gave up and went out to dinner. We found it at 8:50 P.M. and the placenta passed at 9:00 P.M. She let Curt carry it into the barn, but she wouldn't let me near until after it nursed.

I like to watch to see each baby nurse. I know it is important to get the colostrum into the baby within the first 6 hours. If the baby has not nursed by then, I want to be ready to give it some colostrum out of the freezer. I brought my sleeping bag into the barn and settled down in the manger to wait. 12:30 P.M. I woke up and the baby was nursing. I smiled and went back to sleep.

We had chosen to bred Heather to a fairly small Bolivian in order to keep the baby's size down. We did not want a repeat of a 40 pounder. This one was only 35 pounds, still a big girl, but not too big to get out.

Heather is a large brown and white paint. The sire was solid dark reddish brown. Reba came out a deep dark brown that turned to black as she grew. She has a small white mark under her chin. She has beautiful crimped wool that hangs in wavelets. She grew to be a big llama, not small like dad at all. Although she turned out to be a nice llama we decided to not use her dad as a stud in our breeding program. He did not add what we were looking for so we had him gelded.

New cria in coat. Sometimes crias need a little help to get the body temperature up to 101°.

August 16, 1993 Vicky: Komondor Knows Best

Dam's Name:	*Opal*
Baby's Name:	*Vicky*
D.O.B.:	*8/16/93*
T.O.B.:	*9:15 p.m.*
Sex:	*female*
Weight:	*28 lbs*
BoSe:	*yes*
Navel:	*Iodine*
Hernia?:	*no*
Teeth:	*all four*
Heart & Lungs:	*good*
Temperature:	*99.6°*
Weather:	*60° T-Showers*
Problems / Comments:	

It was mid August. We were on the back side of a storm that had rotated back over us. The barometric pressure was shifting rapidly all day. The forecast was for T-storms, but they stayed to the east of us. My fillings hurt all day. Opal was at 338 days and uncomfortable. At about 11:00 A.M., I noticed Opal 's baby was shifting. This usually occurs 10-14 days before delivery, which would have been about right. I had an appointment at the vet's at 1:00 P.M. At noon, I told Curt I would go by myself because I thought Opal was going into labor. Opal is quite fat. She has had false alarms before during previous pregnancies. There was no baby when I got home at four. We had some showers off and on. Curt told me I was being overly alarmist.

Opal was visibly uncomfortable. Maggie, our Komondor livestock guardian dog, began guarding her and wouldn't leave her side. Maggie laid down, tucked against Opal's tail. Curt went outside at 9 P.M. during the TV commercials and found Maggie licking a nose and two feet.

During her previous three births, Opal had delivered standing up, but this time there were lots of ups and downs, mostly downs. When she delivered, she was standing up on the damp sand pile. I kept trying to put a clean sheet under her to keep the baby out of the sand. I was worried about sand getting into the baby's eyes when mom was down. New crias are so pliable as they pass through the birth canal that they seldom get hurt if mom rolls or gets up and down. Never the less, I worry. There is a potential for injury. Baby was out by 9:15 P.M. and nursing by 10:00 P.M. We put nonsteroidal eye ointment in her eyes as an added measure.

The 28 pound baby girl was our only baby by an outside stud. We keep lots of males so we do not use breeding services. We do a few outside breedings each year. In this situation, we had traded services with another farm. It had been very hard to take mom and her baby to another farm for a month.

All dry and fluffed out.

September 2, 1993 Ursala: Dog Bite

Dam's Name:	*Mary*
Baby's Name:	*Ursula*
D.O.B.:	*9/2/93*
T.O.B.:	*daytime*
Sex:	*female*
Weight:	*32 lbs*
BoSe:	*yes*
Navel:	*Iodine*
Hernia?:	*no*
Teeth:	*all four*
Heart & Lungs:	*good*
Temperature:	*100.7°*
Weather:	*90° clear, dry*
Problems / Comments:	*placenta not found*

Ursala's birth was totally routine. We found her at 4:30 P.M. The day was sunny and a dry 90 degrees. She was nursing and doing fine. Curt dipped the umbilical, gave the BoSe and generally checked her over. She weighed 32 pounds. She was a beautiful gray, red, and white paint. Curt was in love at first sight.

We were up early the next day all loaded up and ready to go to State Fair. We do a llama exhibit there each year with several other farms. I went out to check on the new baby before we left. Ursala was sitting with her mother. Susie, one of the mutt pups was sitting near by. Ursala's rear leg was sticking out covered with blood. She had been bitten by my own dog! I screamed. Tears flowing down my cheeks, I ran to get Curt. I can handle most things, but this ripped me up. I had decided to keep the pup. I had hoped she would be wonderful like her mom. I knew she would have to go and I might lose Ursala, too.

Curt thought something had happened to me. I'm allergic to bee stings and he was heading for my bee kit. I tried to tell him what had happened. He ran out to the pasture and I grabbed the first-aid kit. Together we examined the wound. It was about six inches long. The skin had been torn down the back of her hock to her heel, exposing the tendons. The blood vessels were intact. It did not look good, such a big wound for a day old baby. It was too serious a wound for farm first-aid. Curt wrapped it carefully to keep it clean and to prevent further damage. He was worried about the baby going into shock. We put a cria coat on her and Curt carried her to the van.

Lucky for us, it was still early in the morning. We called the vet on his back line and caught him doing early morning rounds in the clinic. He would be ready for us. It takes about 45 minutes to get from our farm to the clinic. Curt would take Ursala, while I would take the truck and trailer to the State Fair.

Setting up the exhibit by myself would be a trick, especially since I had to park in the lot and carry the stuff inside. It was now too late to drive into the barn. I would just have to find someone to help me. It was hard not being able to go to the clinic, but the other farms were counting on us. It was my job that morning to unlock the tack stall and put up the WVLA exhibit and get the video equipment running. It was easier to go myself than to try to get a phone message into the livestock barn.

It was afternoon before Curt arrived at the Fairgrounds. It seemed like forever. Ursala was home, but she was not out of the woods. The tearing was so bad that the skin might not grow back. There might be adhesions on the tendons, causing her to lose some use of the leg. There was danger of infection. She would need daily antibiotic shots. After the initial few days, the wound needed to be cleaned and inspected twice each day. She would need frequent trips to the clinic to trim away dead tissue. She would need to be kept in the barn on stall rest for awhile.

Changing bandages on an active baby is no easy thing. Curt tried putting her in a sling one time. It did not work, but it gave her a hernia. We settled on a body lock. One person sat in the manger with arms, legs, and body wrapped around baby. The other person had to hold the kicking leg and cut the bandage off, check and clean the wound, and rewrap it. We really needed a third pair of hands. The wound was ugly. Circulation to the skin was badly compromised. It took forever to heal.

We got better at the routine. Ursala got a little bit more cooperative, but she always fought. Having the dressing changed was painful. Some days the Telfa pad would stick even though the ads say it never will. Mary was very patient with us. At first she wanted us to leave her baby alone, but after she saw the wound she became more cooperative. Later, when they could be outside, she would always bring Ursala in when we called. She did not accept any nonsense from her baby. All this time, Ursala was growing a pound to a pound and a half a day. Within a month she had more than doubled in size giving us a bigger and bigger baby to wrestle.

It was over a month before we saw any indication of healing. We were worried the rains would come before it healed, adding to our problems. The healing process dragged on. There were setbacks when the vet would cut away dead tissue. It had to be restitched when it tore open. It was an ugly color, but most of that was stain from the betadine used to clean it. Much of the torn skin never reattached. Instead, the wound seemed to grow in from the sides. We expected a horrid scar. We were pleasantly surprised when new skin, and later hair, appeared. We were very pleased that there was no permanent damage to the tendons and that her leg grew equally as strong as the other one.

Ursala stayed with us until she was sold at two years of age. By then there was no visible scar and no limp. She was a very fortunate little llama.

December 10, 1993 Larry: Cold and Stiff

Dam's Name:	*Gail*
Baby's Name:	*Larry*
D.O.B.:	*12/10/93*
T.O.B.:	*btwn 1 and 4*
Sex:	*male*
Weight:	*27 lbs*
BoSe:	*yes*
Navel:	*Iodine*
Hernia?:	*no*
Teeth:	*yes*
Heart & Lungs:	*none*
Temperature:	*hypothermic*
Weather:	*54° 2" rain*
Problems / Comments:	*cold, stiff*

We do not believe in breeding for winter babies. We had planned on breeding this female in March. We had arranged for a farm sitter over Christmas vacation so that we each could go visit our parents. It snowed while we were gone. Our sitter had felt sorry for her favorite male, and put him in the barn with the girls. She had also let our Komondor, who was in heat, out of her kennel. We came home to find our dog pregnant. There had been four open females in the barn, Tammy who is sterile, and three young girls. I called the vet in panic. He came out and examined the girls. It did not look like the youngest two had been bred. Gail was old enough to breed and unrelated to the male. My best course of action was to wait it out. Maggie had a litter of mutt puppies in the barn that spring.

We knew the exact breeding date so we tried to be prepared for another winter baby, hopefully our last. Next time we accidentally end up expecting in December, I'm sending the pregnant mom down south for the birth.

Gary, the young man who helps with the barn, came by and checked her at 12:35 P.M. He picked up her tail. She was eating calmly in the barn. He didn't see any action. He left to take care of his sick mother. I got home shortly before 5:00 P.M. and went straight out to the barn in my school clothes, coat and all. Gail was standing rigid. I found her placenta and began hunting for the baby. She was staring down the hill. Spike was whining a high pitched little hum. I went into Spike's pasture because all the llamas were looking at him. It had rained two inches that day. Mud was pouring down the hill. I was having trouble with my footing in the mud with my school shoes. Spike was standing over what looked like a little mound of wet dung. I finally figured out that was the baby. I was sure it was dead. I couldn't find its' head in the mud. I thought it had been attacked. I picked it up. It was stiff and cold, but it coughed. I ran for the house screaming for help. Curt thought I was a flock of geese flying over the house. Gail followed me to the front door. I took the baby upstairs to the kitchen.

Curt went right to work. The baby had no registrable temperature, no heart and lung sounds, no pupil response, but had an occasional gasp for breath. I called the vet. He was tied up with a dystocia. I asked him to call us every 30 minutes to check our progress. I turned the heat up in the kitchen to about 90. Curt began rubbing the baby with towels and drying him with a hair dryer. We worked and worked. None of our thermometers would register below 90°. The electronic one only flashed below 96° even though the box said it worked down to 90°. The glass ones don't work that low either. We had no way of judging our progress. Gary came in around 6:00 P.M. We put Gail in the barn and I picked up the placenta. About 8:00 P.M., we got him to swallow 2 ounces of warm Pedialite. About 9:00 P.M., the vet called and said to wrap him in plastic bags and put him in the bathtub. We could not get the door off the tub enclosure. That made it a one man job. The bags made him very slippery. It was hard to keep his head up.

115

As he warmed up, he started to squirm, a good sign, but dangerous for a baby wrapped in plastic. We used a candy thermometer to keep track of the bath water temperature. When we took him out, he had to be dried all over again. At 9:30 P.M. I went to Fred Meyers to buy a new thermometer and an electric blanket. Their cash register crashed on overload with the Friday night shoppers. They couldn't process my credit card. I finally wrote a check and left. When I got home, I managed to put baby into a cush position without him falling over. We had him on a polar fleece pad and put the electric blanket over him. Curt went out and milked 2 ounces out of mom. We gave it to baby in a bottle. Baby sucked it right down. At this point we decided to move to the barn.

Gary had tried to clean up the barn. The mud had washed down right through it. The only dry stall was the tack stall. Even it was wet, but not muddy. I dragged the truck bed mat up to the barn and put it on the floor. I moved all the feed and tack out of the stall. I was able to create a 4x8 dry spot in a sea of mud.

I had warmed the placenta up on the kitchen counter. It had been so cold it did not smell. I was sure we would need it. I have saved them for years, but I'd never used one yet, other than to haul it down to OSU for student use.

Gail accepted her baby as soon as we carried him in. We put her in the chute and held him up under her to nurse. Then we put them in the tiny stall. We had planned to put him under the electric blanket to keep him warm since his temperature was only 92°. He wouldn't have any part of it. He was fed up with us and would not cooperate any longer. He wanted to be with mom. We put a polar fleece cria jacket on him. Curt found the electric blanket to be an excellent addition to his sleeping bag in the barn. Curt took first watch and I went to bed. At 2 A.M. the baby nursed on his own. I got up at 5 A.M. and made breakfast. I fed Curt and he went to sleep in the house at 6 A.M.

That afternoon we moved 100 bales of hay out of

the barn so mom and baby could have a dry space. That half of the barn had not been flooded with mud, because the floor was tarpped with the tarp edges wrapped up over the hay. Baby and mom were confined to the barn for the next three rainy days

Baby gained 2 pounds a day for the first week. That is a record for our farm. It shows what breeding for good maternal qualities can do for survival rates. On Sunday baby's ears collapsed. We were afraid to tape them because nighttime temperatures were below freezing. His ears are starting to stand back up. They were not frost bitten. The vet gave Larry a clean bill of health. He is an active, social baby. Little Jim, our preemie runt, sat with him for his first days of barn confinement. Jim could enter that half of the barn through the door of the creep feeder. Larry has a strong preference for Ursala, his half sister, over the other fall babies. He often crawls up on Tammy, my 450 pound sterile female, for naps. She loves it.

We know babies who get such bad starts are more likely than most to have additional problems, but Larry did just fine.

Milk smile peeking around mom.

CHAPTER 9- 1994

A pint sized visitor meets pint sized crias.

March 28, 1994 Anniversary: Running

Dam's Name:	*alice*
Baby's Name:	*anniversary*
D.O.B.:	*3/28/94*
T.O.B.:	*btwn //and noon*
Sex:	*female*
Weight:	*39 lbs*
BoSe:	*yes (4 p.m.)*
Navel:	*Iodine*
Hernia?:	*mild*
Teeth:	*all four*
Heart & Lungs:	*good*
Temperature:	*100.2°*
Weather:	*72° clear*
Problems / Comments:	*placenta not found*

I get choked up when I think of Annie. She died in my arms in the back of the van as we rushed to OSU on Thanksgiving Day. I can still see her body being dragged across the loading dock and into the big cooler at the Diagnostic Lab. We never did get a cause of death. She was eight months old.

Annie was born in the middle of a festive occasion, spring break and our 25th Wedding Anniversary. We had house guests all week. On Sunday we had a big party. The weather was beautiful, clear and sunny all week long. Monday came and it was time for the guests to leave. Curt was at work. I was sick in bed from a migraine that had started the day before from overdoing with all the excitement. My shots had not done the job, so now I was left to wait it out.

Alice was at 349 days. My guests checked on her before they left for the airport. She was fine. She had spent most of the morning under the fir trees where I could see her from my bedroom window. I woke up at noon A big reverse appaloosa cria was running madly about the pasture. Her mom was trying to follow her around. She was still wet and had membrane all over her. I had never seen one come out running like that. There was no way to catch her. All I could do was hope she would slow down long enough to nurse. Everything else could come later.

I did not find the placenta. I was too sick to spend much time looking for it. The dogs finally dragged it in four days later. They had buried it. It was mostly there. I think the dogs had eaten the missing piece.

Eventually Annie got around to nursing. I managed to get a hold of her long enough to dip her navel. She would have to wait until Curt got home for the rest. Annie had a mild umbilical hernia that closed up over the first few weeks on its own.

New baby is checked out by Komondor pups. The pups were raised in the barn to bond them with livestock and make them better working dogs.

April 3, 1994 Lilly: Easter Gift

Dam's Name:	*Irene*
Baby's Name:	*Lilly*
D.O.B.:	*4/3/94*
T.O.B.:	*1:00 p.m.*
Sex:	*female*
Weight:	*32 lbs*
BoSe:	*yes*
Navel:	*Iodine*
Hernia?:	*no*
Teeth:	*all four*
Heart & Lungs:	*good*
Temperature:	*100.8°*
Weather:	*49° sprinkles*
Problems / Comments:	*very fast delivery*

That very same week Curt's high school hosted a class of German students and their teachers. Two of the teachers stayed at our house. They were amazed that we had a farm. They were even more surprised to learn that many teachers in America moonlight in part time and summer jobs. That is unheard of in Germany. I was hoping Irene would have her baby while the teachers were visiting. They took lots of pictures of the llamas and were impressed with Annie.

Sunday came. It was Easter and time change day. We saw our guests off and were home by 1:00P.M. It was starting to sprinkle. We walked out into the pasture to check on Irene. She was just going into labor. We watched it come. This was Irene's fifth baby. The delivery was fast and easy. We were surprised when the little girl weighed 42 pounds. We named her Easter Lilly.

Lilly was a grayish version of her mom, nothing like her Chilibol dad. It did not look like he was adding what we were looking for. Besides, as the stud matured his bite became worse and worse. This guy, too, was out of the stud business.

121

Epidermal Membrane

Crias are covered with a sack like membrane that attaches at all the body openings. None of the openings are closed off, so the sack does not need to be removed. Llama mamas do not lick this off. It dries out in the air and falls off. Occasionally a band will form on an ankle. Do not pull this membrane if it remains attached. Let it dry and trim if necessary. It will usually flake off.

The sheet is an attempt to keep dirt out of new cria's eyes. New babies trash about in the first attempts to try out new muscles. Note the tail wrap and all the grass debris covering mother and cria. Membrane still covers cria.

June 29, 1994 Donald

Dam's Name:	*Ellen*
Baby's Name:	*Donald*
D.O.B.:	*6/29/94*
T.O.B.:	*morning*
Sex:	*male*
Weight:	*27 lbs*
BoSe:	*yes*
Navel:	*Iodine*
Hernia?:	*no*
Teeth:	*all four*
Heart & Lungs:	*good*
Temperature:	*98.5°*
Weather:	*60° sunny, clear*
Problems / Comments:	*floppy ears membranes attached*

The late June weather was clear and sunny at 60 degrees. I looked out the window and saw Ellen with a dark brown cria at about 10:00 A.M. I grabbed the baby box and headed outside. The baby still had membranes attached. I rubbed him down with a towel and dipped the navel in a film can of iodine. I'm getting better at this, not so many orange babies. All four teeth were erupted, but his ears flopped. Baby was trying to nurse, so I backed off and watched. At 11:30 A.M., I checked heart and lung sounds and gave a BoSe shot. By 12:30 P.M. I still was not sure that baby had got a good nursing. I went in and got a warm wash cloth. I put mom in the chute and washed off her utter. I made sure all four quarters were clear and gently pushed baby under mom. He nursed right away with no problems getting him connected. By 4:00 P.M. he had urinated and had a bowel movement. This baby was off to a good start.

August 9, 1994 Kris

Dam's Name:	*Betty*
Baby's Name:	*Kris*
D.O.B.:	*8/9/94*
T.O.B.:	*about noon*
Sex:	*male*
Weight:	*28 lbs*
BoSe:	*yes*
Navel:	*nolvasan*
Hernia?:	*no*
Teeth:	*yes*
Heart & Lungs:	*good*
Temperature:	*99.2°*
Weather:	*72° clear – rain day before*
Problems / Comments:	

Curt found Kris at 1:00 P.M., up and dry. A routine birth, no problems. Curt's notes in the baby book were short and sweet, "Healthy 28 pound boy." Kris was appaloosa like his mom and grandma, with lots of black spots.

The only thing different at all was that we switched from iodine dip to nolvasan. The blue surgical soap was supposed to be better than iodine in that the cord stayed pliable and germs were not sealed in. The umbilical has to be dipped more than once with the blue stuff. That means you have to remember to follow up.

Every spring the WVLA has a Llama Bazaar. It consists of a fun day, educational seminars, and a private treaty sale. Most years Curt and I serve on the organizing committee. The Bazaar is a first class event. It is an excellent place for the newcomer to learn about llamas and see them in action. We find sales such as this one are a good place to sell little males. It can also be a good place for lower end starter animals. In the spring of 95 we took Donald and Kris to the Bazaar.

We arrived at the fairgrounds early because we had so much to do. We had to get our ranch display set up. I had to arrange for the educational seminars, post schedules and posters. Curt was to do a demonstration on carting. When the doors opened to the public, I was still running around trying to get the sound system hooked up. Curt was at our stall. The first man through the doors walked directly up to Curt. He bought Donald and Kris on the spot. Curt talked to him about an hour before he would take the check. Curt wanted to be sure the man had made the right decision.

Curt arranged to deliver the animals. Usually Curt spends about four hours walking around the new living quarters. He checks fences, barns, feeders, and other animals. He looks for possible hazards. He talks about llama care. He instructs new owners to call us day or night if they have any questions or problems

Networking

Your most valuable asset in the llama business is the wonderful people in the industry. Cultivate a llama support network. Join a local association, go to meetings and clinics, participate in activities. Find out who your nearest llama neighbors are and give them a visit. Buy from a local breeder who makes it clear she is willing to help you out day or night. Everyone in the llama industry had to learn from the ground up. We are still finding new answers. Someone out there can answer your questions and provide the support you need.

August 15, 1994 Woodstock: Future Hiker

Dam's Name:	*Heather*
Baby's Name:	*Woodstock*
D.O.B.:	*8/15/94*
T.O.B.:	*afternoon*
Sex:	*male*
Weight:	*34 lbs*
BoSe:	*yes*
Navel:	*nolvasan*
Hernia?:	*no*
Teeth:	*all four*
Heart & Lungs:	*good*
Temperature:	*100.5°*
Weather:	*80° clear*
Problems / Comments:	

My older sister and two of her friends from Girl Scouts arrived in town from California. They were here to attend a wedding of the daughter of another troop member from their elementary school days. They wanted to go for a llama hike in the Cascades. They did not have time for an overnight so it would need to be a day hike.

Curt was sure Heather would have her baby that day. I reminded him that Heather would be a whole lot happier with me gone. He got the honors of baby watch.

Even a day hike needs lots of stuff, especially for four people. I packed a cooler with frozen water bottles, fruit, drinks, snacks. I filled the other pannier with sun screen, bug repellent, first aid kit, stake and line, and some more water bottles to help even the load, a water dish for the llama and a bag of pellets for treats. I threw in wind breakers in case the weather turned. Don't forget TP and trowel. We would stop at the local sandwich shop on the way out of town so everyone could select their own personal preference.

126

I selected Opal Creek as our hiking area. Opal Creek is a gorgeous area of Old Growth forest tucked in between the Bull of the Woods Wilderness and the Jefferson Wilderness. It is an area of controversy because it is not permanently protected from logging. In my opinion it is worth more as it is than clear cut. It serves as the watershed for the city of Salem. Besides, it is not replaceable. There are 500 year old cedar trees, a national treasure. Still people want to log it. Friends of Opal Creek encourage hiking in the area so more people will realize what a treasure it is and demand the area be preserved. Since one of my guests works for the Forest Service, I could not pass up the opportunity. It was my patriotic duty.

We would be taking Spike, a ten year old stud, who hikes well by himself. He usually carries my kitchen so this would be a light load for him. I loaded the Aerostar with Spike, the gear, three 50 year old Girl Scouts, friends for life, and myself. Off we went to the trail head. Curt insisted we take the cell phone. He wanted us to check in as soon as we cleared the canyon on our way home so he could have dinner ready.

We had a terrific time. I had always thought of my sister's friends as being so much older. I had been the tag along little sister. I was pleasantly surprised when they told me how much they had enjoyed having me along. The age difference does not mean much now. Opal Creek was spectacular and cool. The trail is not very steep. The picnic lunch was a hit.

On the way home I remembered to call Curt. Heather had her baby, a 34 pound boy, a paint just like her. My sister named him Woodstock because the second festival was going on. Everything was fine. Dinner would be ready when we got home.

CHAPTER 10- 1995

for the obstacle course.

March 20, 1995 Wanda: Tall and Elegant

Dam's Name:	*alice*
Baby's Name:	*Wanda*
D.O.B.:	*3/20/95*
T.O.B.:	*about noon*
Sex:	*female*
Weight:	*35 lbs*
BoSe:	*yes*
Navel:	*nolvasan*
Hernia?:	*no*
Teeth:	*all four*
Heart & Lungs:	*good*
Temperature:	*99.6°*
Weather:	*45° sctrd showers*
Problems / Comments:	

It was on a very windy day with scattered showers and a warm spring temperature of 45 degrees, that Alice chose to have her sixth baby. Curt spotted the baby at noon, a 35 pound black female. She was still wet. By 12:15 P.M. she was up on her feet. Curt did his usual routine. Mom passed her placenta by 2:00 P.M. It was all very ordinary, a healthy, happy delivery.

Wanda was one of those babies that flops down flat on the ground when she sleeps, just like an old rag. I like to see ears up or some indication of life when I look out in the field. My heart stops every time I see a baby sprawled out like that. It takes about two weeks to a month for babies to firm up.

Curt and I decided to show Wanda in the three ALSA shows we had selected to attend in the summer of 1996. She would be in yearling medium wool class. I think Wanda is beautiful. She is very tall and a nice black color. Too bad she did not impress the judge like she does me. Wanda and I will work on it a bit longer. Llamas, like kids, go through awkward stages as they grow and develop. Maybe we will try

After we had been in llamas a few years, someone asked me why we raised such big llamas. I was startled by the remark. Being six foot tall, I had no idea I had selected big, tall llamas. I just thought they were llamas.

Young crias often spend time together.

April 6, 1995 Mike: Performance Llama

Dam's Name:	*Irene*
Baby's Name:	*Mike*
D.O.B.:	*4/6/95*
T.O.B.:	*daytime*
Sex:	*male*
Weight:	*30 lbs*
BoSe:	*yes*
Navel:	*nolvasan*
Hernia?:	*no*
Teeth:	*all four*
Heart & Lungs:	*good*
Temperature:	*99.0°*
Weather:	*60° rain in a.m.*
Problems / Comments:	

Mike came on April 6. Curt found him about 4:00 P.M. when we got home from work. The day was a little warmer, 60 degrees. It had rained in the morning, but the baby was up and dry. The placenta was already out. Curt did the usual honors. This little guy was solid brown, a little grayer than mom, but not black or woolly like dad.

Mike's mom is one of our best moms. Irene is very protective. She kept him right by her side whenever he was not playing with his buddies. She likes her babies touching her side, not cushed ten feet away. She never goes off and leaves him by himself. She often has all the other babies with her. She'll play with them for hours. It is obvious that Mike inherited both mom's and dad's great dispositions. He is active, friendly, smart and eager to learn.

Mike likes to do the obstacle course. His favorite thing is to stand on top of the big 34 inch high horse jump. He thinks all hay bales left out are for jumping. He never passes on a challenge. If he sees our big guys do something, he's got to do it, too. Chances are he'll want to do it better. He's a big hit with the

Llama Babies

4-H kids that come and practice in our training barn.

I wonder what he will think of costume class. I think he might make a good dragon or a clown or how about a butterfly?

Mom greeting new cria.

May 5, 1995 Pete: Little Stud

Dam's Name:	*judy*
Baby's Name:	*Pete*
D.O.B.:	*5/5/95*
T.O.B.:	*daytime*
Sex:	*male*
Weight:	*33 lbs*
BoSe:	*yes*
Navel:	*nolvasan*
Hernia?:	*no*
Teeth:	*all four*
Heart & Lungs:	*good*
Temperature:	*100°*
Weather:	*50° sctrd showeres*
Problems / Comments:	

May 5 we saw Pete in the pasture, nursing. We went up to check out if it was a boy or a girl, but did not interrupt the nursing. What goes on between mother and cria is a lot more important than what we need to do. Pete was a mostly white appy, not nearly as many spots as his mom and dad. At 33 pounds, chances are he'll grow up to be a big llama, maybe a future packer.

Pete tried mounting mom at two days old. He even had a little orgle. An orgle is the sound males make during breeding. At that point mom was very tolerant of his behavior. Sometimes he would crawl up on her back and fall asleep.

During the summer of 1995 we tried a different marketing idea. We began to take mothers and babies to fairs with us. Selling mother and baby pairs is nothing new. We just had never taken moms and babies with us as part of our exhibit. Pete, Ron, and their moms attended several fairs with us. We were careful to avoid turning it into a petting zoo experience. We never forced the babies to stand and be petted. Pete and Ron adapted well. They played together in the pens, nursed, slept, and watched people. The four llamas were sold as a package towards the end of the summer.

Pete sitting on his mom.

June 30, 1995 Norm: Heat Stress

Dam's Name:	*Nancy*
Baby's Name:	*Norm*
D.O.B.:	*6/30/95*
T.O.B.:	*daytime*
Sex:	*male*
Weight:	*23 lbs*
BoSe:	*yes*
Navel:	*nolvasan*
Hernia?:	*no*
Teeth:	*not erupted*
Heart & Lungs:	*o.k.*
Temperature:	*103° +*
Weather:	*90° clear*
Problems / Comments:	*hyperthermia*

We had eight in a row with virtually no problems at birth. We learned a few things with the next little guy. We had spent the day at the Firecracker Sale. We were not buying or selling this year, but it is a big social event in our local llama community. Friends come to town from all over. Often we have a full house of guests. It had been a 90 degree plus day. People were coming over about 8:00P.M. This time of the year it is light until 9:30 P.M. or 10:00 P.M.

The girls all met me by the gate as I went in the barnyard. I closed the pasture gate so I could show them off when the guests arrived. Someone was doing a lot of humming. It sounded like major distress. I started checking girls. It was Nancy. I gave her a quick look over. Her vulva was enlarged. I started looking for a baby. It could be anywhere. I did not really expect it to be alive, but I wanted to find it, never the less.

I started with the barn, then by the sprinklers under the trees. Next I tried the lower pasture because that was where the girls were when we drove up. I found the cria. It was all the way at the bottom

135

of the hill, flopped up against a fence post, in a heap. Its ears were up, so I knew it was alive. When I picked it up I could tell it was dehydrated. His mucus membranes were dry and crusty. He must have been out in the sun for a long time.

Our guests arrived as I was carrying him up the hill. I tried to stay calm. His body temperature was 103 degrees. I called the vet. Get him hydrated even before trying to get colostrum into him. Use Pedialite, the stuff you give to human babies when they have a fever or diarrhea. I had used it before on puppies. I ran to the store to get some and 5% milk. I started with the Pedialite. The electrolytes are absorbed directly into the system and do not interfere with the digestive track. Tubing a weak and dehydrated cria with any kind of milk may result in the milk just curdling and sitting there.

The Pedialite was like a miracle. We gave it two ounces at a time by bottle since Norm had a sucking reflex. . He perked right up. When his mucus membranes looked hydrated, we switched to 5% milk, still with a bottle to make him work on sucking. Tubing is much easier to do, but it is easier to make a serious mistake. We have never tubed our own crias, but both Curt and I have tubed other people's crias under the vet's instructions. We stuck with the two ounce doses, alternated by Pedialite. When he finally started to try and stand, we gave him two ounces of mother's milk. Actually, he got a bit more because we did not want to waste anything. I have a special wide mouthed plastic measuring cup we milk with. Don't ever use glass, it can break.

Eventually, he was hydrated enough to stand. We did not want to waste time with him trying to find mom. We put her in the chute and held him up to the milk bar. He got the point on about the second try. Because he still needed extra fluids the next day, we continued to give him supplemental feedings of Pedialite. The stuff is like sports drinks, when your body needs it, you don't mind the taste. He drank it right down. Norm proved to be tough. He had a real will to live.

Breeding Logs

Keeping accurate breeding records is a good thing. Knowing when to expect a baby can make it easier to plan your life and reduce unnecessary anxiety. Your veterinarian will want to know breeding dates when doing pregnancy checks. The information is helpful when planning vaccinations and worming dates. My own vet does not vaccinate or handle llamas unnecessarily during the last two months of pregnancy.

The easiest way to keep track of breeding dates when you have a few llamas is to record all dates on a calendar. We started out this way. Be sure to mark down any days a male gets out. As herd size increases, a more complex system may be required if more than one llama is being bred at the same time. I record breedings in a spiral notebook, one page per female. Curt does not like this because he can not rearrange the girls in his preferred order. It works for me, but I see his point. There are herd management programs available for computers or you can adapt an appointment calendar program.

Whatever you do, avoid little loose pieces of paper. They will get lost. You will assume your spouse took care of a breeding and it did not happen. You will get mixed up. Loose little papers or even trying to leave it to memory may lead to disaster, or at least, confusion.

I like to project baby watch dates. I count ahead 350 days. I then target 340 to 360 days. Sometimes it is hard to know just which breeding took. When in doubt, record them both.

Length of gestation data is another good thing to know. After each cria arrives, count back how many days that baby took from breeding to delivery. Record this piece of information for each female each time she delivers. Look for a pattern. Knowing length of previous gestations can help you make predictions or determine if a baby is premature.

July 20, 1995 Ron: Gary in Charge

Dam's Name:	*Ellen*
Baby's Name:	*Ron*
D.O.B.:	*7/20/95*
T.O.B.:	*midday*
Sex:	*male*
Weight:	*31 lbs*
BoSe:	*7/25*
Navel:	*iodine*
Hernia?:	*no*
Teeth:	*yes*
Heart & Lungs:	*good*
Temperature:	*99°*
Weather:	*clear, warm*
Problems / Comments:	

During 1995 Curt made numerous trips to be with his dying parents After his mom died in February, his dad began to decline. Curt spent a total of eight weeks in Palm Springs with his dad. I had to learn that whatever I could do had to be enough. I did not have time for ultra sounds. Some of the girls were pasture bred. I stopped taking outside breedings and sent ten llamas home. I made a few trips south myself for family meetings and moral support.

I had to leave Gary, our ranch hand in charge. He lives just down the road. He takes care of his grandparents' farm, an emu farm, a small horse set up, our llamas, and his own 5 acre farm. He has some of everything, because we all have given him animals. He also likes to go to the local auction, no telling what he'll get. We are very lucky to have Gary after Eric got married, had kids and had to have a real job. Gary sets his own hours and does what he thinks needs doing. I had to adjust my thinking to that. He is very reliable. He comes every day. He even brings his friends and puts them to work.

Curt left for Palm Springs right after our local

Marion County Fair. I put off going for a week, hoping Ellen and Betty would deliver. They would not cooperate. I left for the airport at 4:00 A.M. on July 20. I would drive back with Curt and get home on the 25th. I had Gary watch a birthing video. Llamas are not much different from horses, cows, sheep, and goats. He had done all those. His grandmother is a pediatric nurse as well as farmwife. She said she would check up on any births that might occur while I was gone. I left Gary with the vet's phone number and instructions to call our answering machine everyday.

Wouldn't you know it, by the time I called Gary from the Ontario Airport Ellen had her baby, a 31 pound boy, all black except for a white tip on his tail. Everything was fine.

Trying to stand. At first the cria's legs are extended far out the back. Do not try to judge conformation at this point.

July 24, 1995 Terry: Gary Delivers

Dam's Name:	*Betty*
Baby's Name:	*Terry*
D.O.B.:	*7/24/95*
T.O.B.:	*1:00 p.m.*
Sex:	*male*
Weight:	*24 lbs*
BoSe:	*7/25*
Navel:	*iodine*
Hernia?:	*no*
Teeth:	*2 - barely*
Heart & Lungs:	*good*
Temperature:	*100°*
Weather:	*clear, warm*
Problems / Comments:	

On our way home driving north on I-5 we got a message from Gary. He'd finally seen a llama be born. Betty had her baby, a black woolly male with a white tuxedo front. Gary must have followed her around the entire time we were gone. He weighed 24 pounds. No problems.

Gray's grandmother and most of his extended family had to come see the new baby, Terry. Of course she came as much to share Gary's excitement as to check up on him.

The next day we got home and rushed to see our new crias. We gave them BoSe shots, listened to heart and lung sounds, weighed them, checked for hernias and teeth. Both babies were doing just fine without us.

Gary felt like a real llama farmer, knowing that he could handle llama births. He told me the best thing was knowing that we trusted him enough to leave him in charge. I had not known how important that was to him until he told me.

August 11, 1995 Debbie: Opal Comes Through Again

Dam's Name:	*Opal*
Baby's Name:	*Debbie*
D.O.B.:	*8/11/95*
T.O.B.:	*unknown*
Sex:	*female*
Weight:	*26 lbs*
BoSe:	*yes*
Navel:	*nolvasan*
Hernia?:	*no*
Teeth:	*yes*
Heart & Lungs:	*good*
Temperature:	*101.5°*
Weather:	*clear, warm*
Problems / Comments:	

We discovered Debbie on a Saturday morning. She was either born during the night or the previous day. Curt thinks she was born on Friday and we just missed her. She was totally dry, running around and nursing. She had a few pieces of sack, dry and flaky, on one leg. We never did find the placenta. The dogs might have buried it or the buzzards might have eaten it. Thank goodness for good healthy moms. We dipped her navel in nolvasan, gave a BoSe shot, took her temperature, weighed her and listened to heart and lung sounds, checked for hernia and teeth. She passed all the tests. Debbie is a dilute cream colored llama with little gold spots on her checks. She is not visibly appy like mom nor dark brown like dad.

Debbie is bound to be a good solid breeding female like her full sister Gail. We have been pleased with the combination of large mom and athletic dad. The sire's genes for being thinner are a real plus to Opal's size. Debbie's personality are an improvement over Opal's as well. A good breeding program produces offspring that are an improvement over both dam and sire. In Debbie we have done just that.

Llama Babies

Because Debbie is a plain, no frills llama, we will probably sell her as a three in one package after she has her first baby. Young mother baby packages are attractive to many people because there is less risk involved. You can see what you are getting. Buying an already bred back female means not dealing with a stud or a stud service for another year. The buyer gets the fun of having a baby llama around and none of the hassles of dealing with a stud.

Baby in cria coat.

September 9, 1995: Sara

Dam's Name:	*Heather*
Baby's Name:	*Sara*
D.O.B.:	*9/9/95*
T.O.B.:	*early morning*
Sex:	*female*
Weight:	*29.5 lbs*
BoSe:	*yes*
Navel:	*nolvasan*
Hernia?:	*no*
Teeth:	*four*
Heart & Lungs:	*good*
Temperature:	*99.2°*
Weather:	*58° clear*
Problems / Comments:	

Sara was discovered at 7:00 A.M. It was a pleasant 58 degrees on a clear September morning. She was a beautiful black with white sox, muzzle and throat. This was the second black baby for Heather, a mostly white paint. Everything was fine with this birth. We were pleased to see her weigh in at under 30 pounds, still remembering the fate of her 40 pound sister.

In our years with llamas we have not participated in many ALSA shows. The Oregon State Fair included an ALSA show for the first time in 1995. Our entry took first place in Heavy Wool Adult Male. That may surprise anyone who knows we raise medium to short wooled performance llamas. We do not do shows during the school year because we do not have enough time for travel and preparation. However, Curt got bitten by the show bug. He really has his eye on Get of Sire. He selected four offspring, two males and two females to show at three ALSA shows in the summer of 96. Sara is so striking, she was his first choice.

At home Sara is a mama's girl. She may be weaned,

but she scarcely leaves her mother's side. They cuddle together and are generally best friends. It was hard to teach her to lead if mom was anywhere in sight. I worried how she would do traveling to shows and how she would do in the ring. Sara does not seem to mind travel. She seemed content being stalled with her sister, next to her two brothers and dad. On strange territory she leads and does all the things she would not do at home.

I had not counted on the fact Sara likes to show off. She was terrific in the show ring, a natural, flirting at all the right moments. She had just the right bounce in her step. She did not get bored or space out like some youngsters, but stood attractively at attention when required. I do not know what Curt will say if anyone inquires to buy her.

Curt and his crew placed third in the Get of Sire at COLA. Not bad for a first effort.

Other females in the herd greet the new cria.

Sept. 23, 1995 Frankie: Blue Eyes and Heart Murmur

Dam's Name:	*Mimi*
Baby's Name:	*Frankie*
D.O.B.:	*9/23/95*
T.O.B.:	*6:30 p.m.*
Sex:	*male*
Weight:	*25 lbs*
BoSe:	*yes*
Navel:	*nolvasan*
Hernia?:	*no*
Teeth:	*yes*
Heart & Lungs:	*murmur*
Temperature:	*100°*
Weather:	*warm, sunny*
Problems / Comments:	*large heart defect*

Frankie provided the key to our heart murmur question and marked the end to the breeding career of one of our studs. Frankie's birth was totally normal. He arrived at 6:30 P.M., no problems. Upon examination we noticed he had one blue eye and one white eye. Next, we discovered a monster heart murmur. Frankie nursed fine. However he did a little more mouth breathing than he should. He spent a lot more time sitting with mom than running and playing with the others.

We decided that was easier on mom to let him be with her rather than put him down right away. We weaned him with a group of about five little males. He had his friends and seemed to do fine. Spring was very late in coming. We had freezing nights right into May. I put off shearing my two little Shetland sheep well into June. Finally we had a hot day. The sheep live at our training barn with the little boys. They had to be sheared.

Curt and I had never sheared sheep although we had watched it done many times. How hard could it be? We do llamas. It was a three ring circus. Those

145

two little guys fought and fought. Putting them on their butts or back did not slow them down. The llamas watched with interest. Our big male came and stood right over us to watch. I did a terrible job and never did get their belly wool. We decided to take a break and have a sandwich. When we got back in 30-40 minutes Frankie was dead. Too much stress between the heat and the excitement.

Frankie's body went to Dr. Karen Timm and her anatomy class at OSU. Because of the warm weather we had to haul him to the Diagnostic Lab that night and put him in the big cooler. There was no need of a necropsy, we knew the cause of death. He would serve a better purpose contributing to the educations of future vets.

Mother and still wet cria in the barn.

Weaning

Weaning can be traumatic for everyone, farmer, mom, and baby. There is no one right way. Each farm has to work out what works best given the facilities available and the personalities of the llamas involved.

Some farms leave weaning up to mom. Usually by 8 months of age, mom will wean her cria herself. Some moms will never wean a baby and will let them nurse forever, robbing the next baby of any chance to get adequate colostrum.

Male babies should be removed from the maternity herd at 6 to 8 months of age. Leaving them past a year may result in unwanted breedings. It is easiest to separate these little guys when there are more than one. In our area, breeders often combine singletons of similar age from different farms to provide companionship.

For female babies it is often easier to remove mom from the maternity herd and leave baby with her friends and aunties. Yearling females should be removed from mom's pasture at least two months before mom's next due date. This prevents the yearling from interfering with colostrum production. If last year's baby is already weaned, across the fence should work.

Mom and weanling baby need to be housed farther apart than just across a fence. Mothers and crias are very creative in figuring out ways to nurse through a fence or gate.

Weaning is a very dangerous time for young llamas. Accidents happen. These little guys do dumb things trying to get back to mom. Do not isolate them. They need to be with other llamas. An older gelding or sterile female makes a good nanny.

Weaning is stressful. Do not do it during hot weather or when the temperatures drop to freezing. The youngster may suffer from dehydration from not drinking enough water.

Sept. 26, 1995 Vince: First Wooly Baby

Dam's Name:	*Linda*
Baby's Name:	*Vince*
D.O.B.:	*9/26/95*
T.O.B.:	*daytime*
Sex:	*male*
Weight:	*31 lbs*
BoSe:	*yes*
Navel:	*nolvasan*
Hernia?:	*no*
Teeth:	*all four*
Heart & Lungs:	*good*
Temperature:	*99.2°*
Weather:	*warm, sunny*
Problems / Comments:	

We found Vince when we got home from work. He was up and running around. Linda was swollen and reluctant to nurse. We put her in the chute and applied warm compresses to her udder. Curt milked out her wax plugs. We got the swelling under control. The baby was nursing by 8:00 P.M.

Vince was a cute, black, fluffy guy with bangs. He was a very active baby. A real handful for his first time mom.

Vince also made the A+Llama first string show team. We thought he should show in the wooly class. When we got to COLA we had sense enough to ask the judge. Vince had to show in medium wool, fluff, bangs, and all. In Central Oregon wooly means about three times as much wool as anywhere else in the country.

Vince is now working on learning to do obstacles. His training will include PR and costume, too. Someday he will make a terrific PR llama.

When it was time to wean our 1995 boys, we moved them all up to the training barn where we have more space. They are totally out of sight of the female herd. Chaucer, our old arthritic stud, lives at the training barn because it is flat and he can stay inside if he wants. At first we thought we would keep the little boys separate from Chaucer. He had slowed down so much, we thought they would bother him. We were surprised to discover that Chaucer likes the little boys. He takes his job as nanny very seriously. He does not allow them to fight. His little group expanded to include a pair of two year olds. Chaucer does not allow them to pick on the little guys. Simply a lift of the nose ends all nonsense. Chaucer is doing much better now that he has a job again.

New cria stretched on ground after birthing. Mom is checking her out.

Oct. 18, 1995 Wayne: Last Baby of 95

Dam's Name:	*Karen*
Baby's Name:	*Wayne*
D.O.B.:	*10/18/95*
T.O.B.:	*daytime*
Sex:	*male*
Weight:	*31 lbs*
BoSe:	*yes*
Navel:	*nolvasan*
Hernia?:	*slight*
Teeth:	*yes*
Heart & Lungs:	*good*
Temperature:	*102°*
Weather:	*dry 60°*
Problems / Comments:	

Our last 95 baby came in mid October. The weather was still nice, around 60 degrees and dry. We got home around 6:00P.M. to find Karen's baby boy up, dry and nursing. Curt checked him over and did the routine. Wayne had a slight umbilical hernia which was to disappear on its own in about a month. Wayne looked a lot like Vince except Wayne was dark brown and bigger.

It is great to have babies close enough together that they have playmates. I love to watch the babies run and chase up and down our hill. I am so glad we have big pastures with plenty of room.

At feeding time, the moms usually leave the babies outside to play while moms take care of the serious business of eating. I admire their good sense. The barn feels awfully crowded when the girls are shoving for pellets. We divide the ladies up into different groups to cut down on the spitting and shoving. Pushy llamas are separate from shy ones.

This last group of fall babies were put on vitamin D supplement. We use a paste in a big tube with an applicator that looks like a grease gun. Vitamin D prevents rickets and angular limb deformities. We are careful to follow the vet's instructions because too much vitamin D causes problems, too. It is used here in the Pacific Northwest because we get too little sunshine in the winter.

Curt drying off cria and checking vitals.

CHAPTER 11- 1996

March 19, 1996 Ruth: First 96 Spring Cria

Dam's Name:	*alice*
Baby's Name:	*Ruth*
D.O.B.:	*3/19/96*
T.O.B.:	*daytime*
Sex:	*female*
Weight:	*35 lbs*
BoSe:	*yes*
Navel:	*nolvasan*
Hernia?:	*no*
Teeth:	*yes*
Heart & Lungs:	*good*
Temperature:	*99°*
Weather:	*60°*
Problems / Comments:	

Ruth was another wonderful normal birth. She was black with a white chin. She was up dry and nursing when we pulled into the driveway. I could not find the placenta. Around our house, between the dogs and the buzzards, placentas do not last long if they are out in the open. Curt did his usual routine. Ruth weighed 35 pounds.

Waldo, our Komondor mutt, dug up the placenta the next day. I took it away from him and put it in the trash. It was too late to inspect it for wholeness. We have never had a retained placenta, so I may be a little lax about this. We do watch moms for discharge, even if we find the placenta in good shape.

Ruth is great friends with her big sister, Wanda. Female llamas develop life long bonds between mothers and daughters, sisters, and playmates they grow up with. Consecutive sisters have a very special relationship. Ruth follows Wanda around. She grazes with her. They take dust baths together. In the evenings, Wanda runs and plays with Ruth and her little friends.

Llama Babies

Curt likes to call Ruth Milk Mouth. I do not approve of the nickname. It is not positive enough. Since I am the one that fills out the ILR forms, the nickname will not be around for long.

Ruthie has special status in our herd. She is the oldest and largest of our spring/summer babies. Her mother, Alice, is the dominant female in our herd. Alice inherited the job from her mother when Gretchen became ill. Alice is not the oldest or the biggest by weight. She is the tallest female in our herd along with her younger sister.

When Ruthie was about two days old, her mother and some other adult females taught her to run. The adults formed a circle and chased Ruthie back and forth between them. They chased her faster and faster while moving further apart. Soon Ruthie could run as fast as the grown ups.

Ruthie and the other young llamas love to run and play. Every evening just before dusk, the little ones begin to play. They leap, bounce, and twist. My favorite is to watch them all in a line, with Gretchen in the lead, pronking across the hillside. Like a Bunny Hop chain at New Years, Gretchen gathers up all the little ones and most of the adults and off they go.

When the moon is full, the entire herd will join in the dance. They will run and leap in the moonlight for hours.

Pronk

This word is hard to find in the dictionary. It refers to one of the natural gaits of llamas. A pronk is a bounce with all four feet off the ground at the same time. It is used in play and in evading predators.

ILR

The International Lama Registery known as the ILR is an important service to llama breeders. For the last ten years, most llamas and alpacas in the United States are registered and assigned an identification number. The ILR maintains genealogical records on llamas and supplies registration certificates. Any llama purchased in the U.S. should come with a registration certificate. Unregistered llamas should not be bred. Their offspring cannot be registered. They can not be shown in ALSA Shows.

Forms and information can be obtained directly from the registry. The address of the ILR is:

International Llama Registry
PO Box 8
Kalispell MT, 59903

Livestock guardian pup at the barn.

April 7, 1996 Candy: Daddy's Girl

Dam's Name:	*Gail*
Baby's Name:	*Candy*
D.O.B.:	*4/7/96*
T.O.B.:	*early morning*
Sex:	*female*
Weight:	*32 lbs*
BoSe:	*yes*
Navel:	*nolvasan*
Hernia?:	*slight*
Teeth:	*yes*
Heart & Lungs:	*good*
Temperature:	*99.2°*
Weather:	*60° sprinkles*
Problems / Comments:	

We found Candy at 8:00 A.M. Sunday morning. She was up, dry and nursing. Curt did the usual procedures. He found a slight umbilical hernia. These things usually close up by themselves very quickly. Candy's took about a month to disappear. She is reddish brown like her daddy, not cream like mom, Gail.

Candy, Vera, and Ruth love to run and play. The three little girls pal around together. They can run up and down our hill even on the hottest days. They love to run in and out of the sprinklers when it is hot. Sometimes Timmy and Precious join in the romp. Pedestrians had better watch out when the pack of five whizzes by.

Our vet comes for herd health in June right after school gets out and again in December during Christmas break. We weigh everyone and trim tornails the day before. We have the vet do wormings, vaccinations, a brief physical of each animal, and pregnancy testing. This year Candy and Vera were too young for their vaccinations, so the vet left them with me to do later.

When later came, I had to get Curt to help me

give the shots. I had not done my usual halter training, so both babies were wildly leaping around when I needed them to stand.

I try to start halter training at about 3 to 4 months. I start by rounding up the mothers and babies into the barn. First I catch the babies and put the halters on them. I let them run around with the halters on for 10 to 15 minutes, then I take the halters off. I repeat this step several days. Next, I add a short lead to the halter and let the baby drag it around for 10 to 15 minutes while I watch and make sure they do not get into trouble. I may need to repeat this lesson up to three times. Then, I borrow a step from John Mallon. I tie a bike inner tube to the barn wall. I halter the baby and tie the lead to the inner tube. The inner tube acts as a shock absorber. The little one will bounce around until it tires of fighting. I watch safely out of harms way. Curt prefers to be a human shock absorber. He hangs onto the lead himself and drags the little guys up and down the driveway. It might be that they drag him. Finally, I take the baby for a walk with its mother.

Doing some training before weaning reduces stress. The baby can still run back to mom and be comforted after each session. Baby can accompany mom for some training. Baby gets the message, "This is what llamas do."

April 9, 1996 Vera: Sweet and Healthy

Dam's Name:	*Irene*
Baby's Name:	*Vera*
D.O.B.:	*4/9/96*
T.O.B.:	*daytime*
Sex:	*female*
Weight:	*34 lbs*
BoSe:	*yes*
Navel:	*nolvasan*
Hernia?:	*no*
Teeth:	*yes*
Heart & Lungs:	*good*
Temperature:	*99.4°*
Weather:	*60° sprinkles*
Problems / Comments:	

Tuesday was a cloudy day with sprinkles and temperatures in the mid sixties. Vera was up and nursing when we got home at 4:45 P.M. She is rather dark gray with a white halo effect. I am sure she will change color to some sort of brown later on. Not many llamas stay gray. Curt did the honors. We were thankful for another healthy baby on the ground.

Curt has a story he tells about the day Vera was born. He stopped to pick up the mail at the bottom of the hill. When he looked up at the house, he saw buzzards circling in the sky over the upper girls' pasture. He was afraid something had died. He drove up the hill and pulled into the driveway a little fast. He almost hit something big and black, flapping wildly in the lane. It was a big buzzard dining on placenta, a bit too full to get out of the way of the speeding truck. Waldo and Raven, the dogs, were up in the pasture guarding the newest addition to our llama family.

Vera is quiet and sweet like all of Irene's babies. I expect she will grow up to be friendly and confident with a great disposition. I hope we get to keep her.

We have sold all of Irene's babies. People fall in love with them.

Irene is a great mom. She usually has two or three babies with her. They all follow her around. She is the mama llama in charge of babies. Irene joins in when the babies play. I think she does it just to keep an eye on her own youngster.

Irene is also Ms. Manners. She insists on quiet behavior in the barn and respect and courtesy towards elders. She must have been a school teacher in another life.

Sweet llama baby.

June 6, 1996 Tim: Ladies' Man

Dam's Name:	*Patty*
Baby's Name:	*Tim*
D.O.B.:	*6/6/96*
T.O.B.:	*daytime*
Sex:	*male*
Weight:	*32 lbs*
BoSe:	*yes*
Navel:	*nolvasan*
Hernia?:	*no*
Teeth:	*yes*
Heart & Lungs:	*good*
Temperature:	*99.2°*
Weather:	*85° sunny*
Problems / Comments:	

On June 6 Patty delivered her first baby, a 32 pound boy. Everything went as it should. We put a list of possible names up on the bulletin board, but one did not pop out right away. We do not have a system of naming our herd. Usually we pick something with some sort of connection to mom's name, something that suits the personality, or something related to an event surrounding the birth. Many names have A+Llamas included. We have A+ as our herd identifier. In the meantime Curt calls all new babies Precious. Patty's baby looks so small next to the spring babies that I started calling him Tiny Tim. He's going to be a big llama so that name won't fit for long. Maybe Tim the Tool Man Taylor.

Timmy is a real ladies man. Currently he is the only male baby in the maternity herd. All the other boys are in the little boys' pasture at the training barn. He runs and chases with the three bigger spring girls. The four of them, all solid colored, range from browns to black. When they tire out, they all crash on the sand pile. Timmy tries mounting the girls, but he usually gets tired, snuggles up and goes to sleep.

Timmy was happy when Precious came along. She is bigger than him, but he is much more careful in playing with her than he is with the bigger girls. She is his pal. Together they explore the world.

Baby may fall several times trying to take its first steps.

June 24, 1996 Opal's Abortion: Chapters Happen

June 24 started out as an ordinary Monday. We had thunder clouds and rain showers for the last two days. We had done herd health on Friday. Panacur, 7- way, tetanus toxoid for all. TB tests and blood tests for five animals going to an ALSA show in Washington. One gelding for a retired stud. Preg checks for the girls, rectals or ultrasounds. Two of the girls, due in July, had to pass because they were too close to their due dates to risk examination. Those with September and October due dates were included. Nobody was due in August this year. The vet would be back out on Monday afternoon to check on the TB tests.

Two young females I had tried to breed last summer were open. My three oldest girls did not carry through the long, hard winter. Also one October breeding did not take. Six open females. Pretty tough. We do not do breedings in November, December, January or February. Usually we do about a third of our herd in March, however this year winter was still pouring out of the sky. Everything was put on hold. It is too difficult and dangerous to do breedings in knee deep mud. Tana and Gretchen no longer have annual babies. Vicky and Reba just were not ready. Karen and Mary were a disappointment. Had it been a normal year, I would have caught that in March. If llamas were still a big money thing, I would have been devastated. Instead, I took it in stride. Considering the year, there was absolutely nothing else I could have done, nothing I had the resources to do differently. I was relieved to know that any of them were pregnant. Loosing both of Curt's parents had disrupted the routine on our farm.

The vet arrived at 2 o'clock Monday afternoon. Curt called the girls down. He shut the barn as soon as he had the two he wanted. Not all the girls came down. Some were standing under the trees to get out of the rain. Today Curt and the vet would drive up to the other barn to check TB tests on the boys. We did not need the chute, so we did not bring them

162

down to the girls' barn. Our non breeding males live at our training barn.

As the men left, Waldo began to bark. He was up in the girls' pasture. His bark sounded strange. I walked up the hill. Waldo was guarding an aborted fetus lying in a heap under the fir trees. It looked about nine months along. This was the first time I ever had an abortion like this. Who's baby was it? I picked it up. Most of the placenta was attached. Opal moved toward me and hummed. She turned away. I could see her vulva was swollen and sore. It was the size of my hand. The fetus was cold and wet, still covered in membrane. The head drooped over my arm as I walked towards the house. Mom didn't follow me. I swore softly at myself as I walked down the slippery mud. If I had not insisted on the preg checks would this baby still be safe and alive inside mom today? I could tell by mom's swelling that the delivery had been hard.

The tears were gone by the time I reached the house. There was work to do. I placed it on the kitchen counter. I got out a cardboard box and some plastic bags to pack it in. I called the vet clinic and asked the receptionist to call the vet on his car phone and tell him to come back to the house. Opal needed to be examined. I took a halter and lead from its hook in the laundry room and returned to the pasture. Opal did not want to be caught. She kept returning to the place where her baby had laid on the ground. Raven, our other dog, brought me part of the placenta. I put it in a plastic bag in my pocket. Eventually I herded her back to the barn.

Curt put Opal in the chute. Dr. Long washed her off with iodine swabs. He checked the small tear at the top of her vulva. He checked her vagina for tears. Everything looked good except for the swelling. He examined the placenta. It was a dark purplish brown, not a normal color.

We went into the house to examine the fetus. It was a white appy male. This time Murphy's Llama Law did not work. This little white male did not make it. We had been trying for a good packer. We came close. Much of the placenta was still attached to the baby. The placenta was the wrong color and had edema. Hair was sloughing off the fetus. It had been dead several days. It would need to go to the lab at

Meeting a new friend.

OSU for something called an abortion screening. A blood sample from the dam needed to be included. Dr. Long warned that 70% of the cases sent to the lab get no results.

Pregnant women, women of child bearing years, and children should never handle aborted fetuses or placentas because of the danger of catching and spreading an infectious disease that causes miscarriage. I got a thorough lecture for picking up the fetus without gloves and for putting it on the kitchen counter. I would normally have used the laundry room counter, but the laundry was on it. I scrubbed everything down with antibacterial cleaner twice. My clothes were soaked in fluids. Those went into the laundry and were washed twice. Then I showered off with antibacterial soap.

Opal would need daily penicillin shots until the results came back. She would need a vaginal exam before being rebred. Since everything looked like it all came out, she did not need any further examination today.

Saturday the lab results were on the answering machine. Leptospirosis. The entire herd would need to be vaccinated. The winter's mud had taken its toll. This disease is passed through urine. It can be spread by standing water, either by drinking it or by getting it into a cut or scrape. Our girls have plenty of clean water to drink from automatic waterers. We had standing water all winter from the floods. We had taken some animals to shows this spring. We also have deer that come onto our property to graze occasionally. The deer mostly stay in the cherry orchard above us, but we had more than our share of runoff this year. Rodents are another possible source. Our cat tries hard to keep up with them, but every barn has its mice. We might never know the source, but it is our job to eradicate the disease from our farm.

We had to vaccinate the entire herd and give boosters again in one month. After that, they will get shots every six months for two years.

June 26, 1996 Precious

Dam's Name:	*Nancy*
Baby's Name:	*Preciouys*
D.O.B.:	*6/26/96*
T.O.B.:	*1:00 p.m.*
Sex:	*female*
Weight:	*38 lbs*
BoSe:	*yes*
Navel:	*nolvasan*
Hernia?:	*no*
Teeth:	*yes*
Heart & Lungs:	*good*
Temperature:	*99.6°*
Weather:	*71° sunshine*
Problems / Comments:	*shortened cord*

Two days later on the 26th, Nancy had a baby girl. Nancy is a big llama and her baby weighed 38 pounds. She came out looking bigger than Timmy. She is a red and white paint with white neck and front legs, a beautiful baby. She is very athletic, a trait she got from dad, not couch potato mom. She loves to run and leap. It did not take her a week to figure out that some of the other aunties were more fun to play with than her mom. She is the first baby to start playing and the last one to stop.

When Precious was born, her umbilical cord was longer than it should be. I was afraid she would step on it and tear it. It needed to be trimmed. We have wide dental floss soaked in iodine for this purpose. I held the baby while Curt tied off the cord in two places, careful not to get it too short. Then he cut off the excess cord. There was membrane from the sack still attached to the cord. Curt carefully trimmed that as well.

It was such a relief to have this baby come out healthy after going through the abortion with Opal. It felt good to be able to refocus on this positive new life. We have one more baby to worry about. The rest should be covered by the vaccinations.

When people come over to see our babies the first thing they say is, "Oh, how nice. She isn't dark." I guess all those solid colored dark babies do get a little boring. We had so many white ones. I do like the paint, and the appy, and the brown, and the black, and the white. I like them all, healthy, happy llama babies playing in my pasture.

Certainly the best thing about llamas is the babies.

A paint cria still wet from birth.

167

Lisa's Baby

We bought Lisa at a herd dispersal auction. We bought her as an open female to breed to a brand new stud. When we got her home, it turned out she was pregnant. She had been bred at 13 months. She did not carry the pregnancy. She had a series of infections and stopped cycling. We did not have any recourse because it had been a buyer beware type sale with no guarantees. Besides the breeder was dead. That made things rather final.

We tried for two years to get her bred. Finally I just put her in with a male for pasture breeding. Sometimes llamas know what to do better than people do. Lisa got pregnant.

With pasture breeding you do not have the exact breeding date so baby watch gets prolonged, sometimes to a month or more. With a first time mom you do not know what to expect. You have no breeding records to compare length of gestation. With a mom from outside your herd you may not know anything about how her mom, sisters and grandmother did with their pregnancies. We knew less about Lisa's previous life than any other llama we had owned. We took a big risk buying her without that kind of information. Would the risk pay off or would she turn out to be a mistake?

Appendix 1
Baby Box Contents
Here is what I keep in a small ice chest with a top handle and positive latch:
thermometer - digital
thermometer covers
stethoscope
small notebook
waterproof pen
j-lube
KY lubricant
7% iodine
Nolvasan
rubber gloves
OB sleeve
nail file/nail clippers
scissors
alcohol swabs
garbage bags
clean sheet
paper towels
clean towels
wide dental floss in small bottle of iodine
bulb aspirator
film cans for dipping
small plastic bottle for mixing nolvasan
enema bottle
Vet wrap

Keep in refrigerator:
BoSe
Penicillin
colostrum- in freezer section

Keep in medical cabinet
needles and syringes
sharps container
baby bottles
general first aide supplies
Pedialite
Fly spray

Appendix 2
Statistics

Here are some statistics based on the births at A+ Llamas during the time of this book. All the numbers have been rounded to whole numbers.

Total number of babies = 60
Live births = 57   (95%)

Stillbirths and abortions = 3   (5%)

Number of girls = 32   (53%)

Number of boys = 28   (47%)

Number of births needing assistance = 4   (7%)

Number of observed births =18   (30%)

Number of births while away from home = 23 (40%)

Number of births while home = 35   (60%)

Number of daytime births = 48   (80%)

Number of evening births = 5   (10%)

Number of early morning/nighttime births = 6 (10%)

Number of babies needing intervention = 4   (7%)

No maternal deaths.

Average weight gain = 1 to 1 1/2pounds for first month

Average birth weight = 29.8 pounds
(1989-1996, 48 live births)

Appendix 3
Llama Baby Normals

Gestation= 350 days ± 2 weeks

Birth weight= 22 to 38 pounds

Temperature
> Adult= 99 -102°
> Just born cria= same as dam
> Baby = 100 -102.5°

Respirations= 10 - 40 breathes per minute
(Llamas breathe through the nose)

Pulse = 90 -140 beats per minute

Bibliography

Johnson, LaRue W. DVM, *Llama Owners and Dystocia,* Colorado State University.

Smith, Brad DVM, Pat Long DVM, and Pam Reed DVM, *Llama Neonatal Care Seminar,* College of Veterinary Medicine, Oregon State University.

Fowler, Murry E. DVM. *Medicine and Surgery of South American Camelids,* 1989, Iowa State University Press.

Hoffman, Clare DVM. and Ingrid Asmus, *Caring for Llamas and Alpacas, A Health and Management Guide, 1996,* Rocky Mountain Llama Association

A+ Llamas Mission Statement

MISSION

To build a productive, self supporting llama herd with a reputation for honesty, dependability, and fairness. To sell solid production females and excellent performance males. To supplement our income and insure our future retirement. To enjoy our llamas and farm. To coordinate our llama activities with our full time careers.

OBJECTIVES

- To breed and sell solid production female and performance male llamas with good health, reproductive fitness, conformation, disposition, size, bone, and basic training.

- To offer affordable llamas with personal support to those purchasing our llamas.

- To operate our farm as a successful small business.

- To promote llama education.

- To have fun with our llamas by putting them to good use and being actively involved with doing things with them.

STRATEGIES

To breed and sell solid production female and

*performance male llamas with good health, repro-
ductive fitness, conformation, disposition, size,
bone, and basic training.*

- Male careful selection of the animals used in our breeding program.
- Make careful pairing of animals to optimize positive traits.
- Conscientious herd management practices.
- Regular veterinary care.
- Provide regular training.
- Stay up to date on llama health care information.

*To operate our farm as a s successful small busi-
ness.*

- To make good use of experts such as our accountant, veterinarian, genetics consultant and OSU Vet School staff.
- To keep accurate financial records.
- To keep our farm neat and presentable at all times.
- To develop a business plan including a marketing plan and advertising campaign.
- To set goals.
- To build a reputation of honesty, dependability and fairness.

To promote llama education.

- To learn more about llamas by attending meetings, conferences, seminars, and reading books and magazines.
- To write articles for newsletters.

- To support OSU Vet school and llama research.
- To provide original information sheets at our displays.
- To share information with newcomers.
- To promote and participate in the WVLA and LANA.
- To support low cost seminars.

To have fun with our llamas by putting them to good use and being actively involved with doing things with them.
- To train males to do useful and fun things such as packing and carting.
- To take all males out in public.
- To use wool in spinning and weaving and fiberarts.
- To attend fun days and participate in performance events.
- To invite others to participate with us.
- To support efforts to expand the llama market through more participatory events such as shows, fairs, and fun days

To offer affordable llamas with personal support to the buyer.
- To support the Llama Bazaar and other private treaty sales where we can have direct contact with the buyer.
- To sell off the farm.
- To offer new owner training.
- To provide follow up to all buyers.
- To offer reasonable prices and good value.
- To keep current with the market.

Ten Good Things to Do While Waiting

1. Take a Neonatal Care Clinic.

2. Watch a birthing video.

3. Purchase and read <u>Caring for Llamas and Alpacas</u> by Clare Hoffman and Ingrid Asmus.

4. Collect or update baby box.

5. Send for ILR forms to register baby.

6. Write out your questions and discuss with vet.

7. Find out about previous birthing history or birthing history of mother.

8. Establish your llama network.

9. Visit other farms during birthing.

10. Pick a name.

Index

U

Ultrasound 76
umbilical cord
   8, 84, 166
umbilical hernia 89,
   90, 120

V

vaginal flushing 46
Veterinarian 37
Vitamin D 5,150

W

wax plugs 99
Weaning 147
Willamette Valley Llama
   Association 65
WVLA-OSU Llama Herd
   Health Seminars. 67

ABOUT THE AUTHOR

Barbara Norris Anderson has been active in llamas since 1984. She and her husband, Curt Anderson, own and operate *A+ Llamas* on 22 acres in Salem, Oregon. They have three cats, a house bunny, two dogs, two Shetland sheep, and about 40 llamas. Barbara has a Masters Degree in Special Education and teaches middle school. Curt teaches high school math, computers, and accounting. The Andersons are active members of the Willamette Valley Llama Association.

Llama Babies

LLAMA BABIES:
UP, DRY, AND NURSING

ORDER INFORMATION

Please provide the following information:

Name, address, city, state,zip
Quantity of books desired @ -------- each
Shipping and handling $2 first copy
$1 for each additional copy

Send check or money order to:

A+ Llamas
6138 Inwood Lane South
Salem, OR 97306